THE ROTTWEILER TODAY

JUDY AND LARRY ELSDEN

HOWELL
BOOK HOUSE

New York

Maxwell Macmillan Canada
Toronto

Maxwell Macmillan International
New York Oxford Singapore Sydney

Howell Book House
Macmillan Publishing Company
866 Third Avenue
New York, NY 10022

Maxwell Macmillan Canada, Inc.
1200 Eglinton Avenue East
Suite 200
Don Mills, Ontario M3C 3N1

Macmillan Publishing Company is part of the Maxwell Communication Group of Companies

Library of Congress Cataloging-in-Publication Data

Elsden, Judy
      The Rottweiler today / Judy and Larry Elsden.
            p.   cm.
      ISBN 0-87605-294-4
      1. Rottweiler dog. I. Elsden, Larry. II. Title.
SF429.R7E48 1992
636.7'3--dc20   91-26112
                                                                     CIP

Macmillan books are available at special discounts for bulk purchases for sales promotions, premiums, fund-raising, or educational use. For details, contact:

Special Sales Director
Macmillan Publishing company
866 Third Avenue
New York, NY 10022

10 9 8 7 6 5 4 3 2 1
Printed in Singapore

Contents

ACKNOWLEDGEMENTS

Rottweiler lovers all over the world have helped us to write this book. Any request by us for information, anecdotes or photographs has met with the most generous response. As a result, we have suffered what could be described as an embarrassment of riches and much excellent material has had to be left out for no other reason than a shortage of space. To all those who went to considerable trouble to send us material, we extend our thanks, and our apologies to those whose contributions have not been used.

Our thanks are due to the **Federation Cynologique International**, the **Allgemeiner Deutscher Rottweiler Klub e.V.**, the **American Kennel Club** and the **British Kennel Club** for permission to reproduce the relevant Breed Standards. Also to the **American Rottweiler Club** for permission to include the excellent line drawings by **Pamela Anderson** contained in the A.K.C. Illustrated Standard.

The Royal Army Veterinary Corps Centre was very helpful in interrupting a busy schedule to provide photographs and details of their work.

We are also extremely grateful to **Joan Klem** and **Clara Hurley** for their permission to reproduce the photographs of their dogs and for information on the American Rottweiler scene. To **Gwen Chaney** and the American Rottweiler Club for their help and assistance. We would particularly wish to mention the **Midland and Northern Rottweiler Clubs** along with other **British breed clubs** for their help.

All those busy workers with therapy dogs who took time out from their work to send us details deserve our gratitude, especially **Nigel Tombling** for his description of a P.A.T. dog at work. Our thanks to **Roy Hunter** of **Anglo-American Dog Training**, who described his experience with the first Rottweiler to work with the British civil police.

The Rottweiler is fortunate in having so many supporters throughout the world. Many of them have helped us write this book. Both we and the Rottweiler are grateful to them.

Introduction

We have known and loved the Rottweiler for over thirty years. In Britain during that time we have seen it progress from a breed that no one had heard of to one of the most popular breeds in the world. However, in Britain – virtually without warning – the breed fell from its peak of popularity to a position where it was abused by the media, hated and feared by a large section of the general public and viewed with suspicion by the Government. The Rottweiler found itself as the focal point of a massive campaign against dogs in general and against the "guarding" breeds in particular. As a result, there is now legislation in Britain banning two types of dogs, the American Pit Bull Terrier and the Japanese Tosa, and also any other type bred purely for the purpose of dog-fighting. The legislation also includes the power to order the muzzling and restraint of other breeds considered to be dangerous. While there are no breeds at present on this list, there can be no doubt that in the eyes of some of the public and politicians the Rottweiler should be included.

For those that understand the true nature of the Rottweiler, this is an appalling situation, and although the problem is largely confined to Britain, it must serve as a warning to other countries that have a large population of Rottweilers. The Rottweiler finds itself in this position through no fault of its own. It is still the same wonderful dog that it has always been. However, there are aspects of the breed that can be misused and exploited by man, and this has happened both in Britain and elsewhere. Furthermore, this is not a dog that is suitable for every owner or for every type of home.

Most dog breed books give a rather romantic view of the breed's origins, extol its

A fine representative of Judy and Larry Elsden's Chesara Rottweilers – Ch. Chesara Dark Charles. Top Stud Dog all breeds U.K. 1983. Top Rottweiler Stud Dog 1982 to 1985.   *Pearce.*

virtues, ignore any problems, and then tell you how to raise and train it. In this book, we have tried to examine the Rottweiler in greater depth, looking not only at its virtues, but also at its problems. Much of what it contains is from our own experience of the breed. It also contains a large amount of our own thoughts and opinions, with which you may or may not agree. Either way, we shall have achieved our object if we are successful in making you think about the Rottweiler. We hope that it can play some small part in increasing the understanding of the breed and in ensuring its future, not only in the show ring, but also as a working dog and, above all, as a loved and trusted member of the family.

Chapter One

THE ROTTWEILER

Breeds of dogs take their names from many different sources: they have been named after monarchs, countries, castles, counties and districts, and many are named after their function. The Rottweiler eschews any attempt to describe its function, for this is a multi-purpose dog that is able to undertake a wide range of tasks. The Rottweiler takes its name from the town of Rottweil in Swabia, Southern Germany. This area of Europe had limited and difficult communications, and as a result it produced a number of breeds with similar characteristics, although varying in detail. This was a world of isolated valleys surrounded by high mountains, with the high passes blocked by snow for much of the year, and so the development of a working dog took place in a relatively limited area. Obviously, the basic requirements for working dogs were similar throughout the region, but geography dictated that you had to breed from the dogs in your immediate vicinity. Therefore the Rottweiler evolved in the area of Rottweil, and was named after its birthplace.

The Rottweiler has frequently been called the 'butcher's dog' and much has been made of this description. Ostensibly, the relationship between butcher and dog seems incongruous; they are normally regarded as enemies of each other, and their relationship is usually portrayed by a dog fleeing from a butcher's shop with a leg of lamb in its mouth, hotly pursued by the butcher waving a meat cleaver. However, if you think of a butcher as someone who buys his cattle from distant markets and uses his dog to drive them home, then the term 'butcher's dog' begins to make sense. The term 'drover's dog', sometimes used in old German studies of the breed, is really a far more accurate description.

There is a rather more bizarre explanation for the term 'butcher's dog', which we found when we were looking into the origins of the Boxer. Moral attitudes have changed radically over the centuries, and in more violent times it was actually *illegal* to kill a bull that had not been baited by dogs – a far cry from the outrage that baiting would provoke today. There were two reasons for this seemingly barbarous practice. Firstly, it was to let everyone know that a bull was being killed so that his flesh could not be sold as prime beef. Secondly, it was believed that the meat from an animal killed immediately after violent exercise would be more tender. Baiting was the task of the butcher, and he would keep special dogs for the purpose. Both Boxers and Rottweilers were used for this purpose. Fortunately, both breeds quickly showed that they had many other more attractive qualities.

If you pursue the theory that the original Rottweiler developed as a drover's dog, you are confronted with the fact that both in temperament and physical appearance, it does not conform to the general concept of a herding breed. The most typical dogs of this group are the German Shepherd or the Border Collie. Hans Korn, considered to be one of the doyens of the breed, writing in 1939, points out that the Rottweiler exhibits few characteristics which accord with those of other cattle dogs, and that its psychological make-up conforms much more with breeds like the Boxer – dogs of the broad-mouthed mastiff type, bred for centuries as war dogs, fighting dogs and guard dogs.

In the early days of development, breeds of dogs, or perhaps more accurately types of dogs, tended to reflect their owners' needs, and also their status. The lord in his castle could afford to breed and keep a variety of dogs, each for a different purpose: dogs for coursing, dogs to hunt in packs, dogs to guard his property, and even something small and pretty as a lap-dog for his lady. At the opposite extreme, a peasant economy demands that there are no useless mouths to feed. In order to survive, each individual must work and earn its keep, and they may be required to carry out a wide variety of tasks. Invariably, the breeds of today which combine high intelligence with multi-purpose come from humble backgrounds.

The Rottweiler probably developed from a mixture of native cattle dogs, relatively nondescript in type, modified by the introduction of broad-mouthed dogs, technically of the Mastiff type, but in fact more akin to the original English Bulldog or the German Bullenbeiser. It can be assumed that the broad-mouthed dog was introduced deliberately in order to give the dogs the power to deal with large animals such as bulls. The Rottweiler's prime purpose was to work cattle, to drive them long distances and to guard them when pastured. It had to be able to control an obstinate bull, encourage the more docile stock such as sheep, and exert its will over stubborn and independent-minded pigs. During the long days and nights on the road the Rottweiler would be its master's sole companion – a friend and also a protector.

From the very beginning, this was a dog who lived and worked close to man and who developed a strong affinity with its owner. At home and at rest, the Rottweiler lived alongside the family, playing with the children and guarding them. In the not too distant past, the dog would also would have been used for hunting, using its tracking ability to follow the wild boar, and then holding prey with its powerful jaws and formidable strength until help came. As if all this was not enough, the Rottweiler would also be harnessed to a cart to deliver the wares of butchers, bakers and milkmen.

There were two sizes of Rottweiler. In 1926 the Allgemeiner Deutscher Rottweiler Klub (ADRK) published *The Rottweiler in Word and Picture*, and the author states that there were large heavy dogs used for draft work, and a smaller more agile animal used for working stock. The big, heavy dogs would not have been able to maintain the activity needed to herd stock, and they could also have injured small stock by their weight. The smaller dogs could nip the cattle on their hocks when chivvying them along, while the bigger dogs would have been able to bite on the cattle's shoulder, thus damaging the beast. There is no record of actual measurements, but it is clear that there were considerable differences in both size and weight, which by modern standards would mean classification as two separate breeds or, at least divisions of the same breed. According to *The Rottweiler in Word and Picture*, the two strains were always kept separate and were not interbred. In the larger type, colour was established and maintained, but the smaller dogs frequently carried white markings. As they were bred solely for their working ability, the colour aspect was ignored. We know one German breeder, whose knowledge of the breed goes back for many years, and both he and his father considered that a Rottweiler with a small patch of white on the chest would be more intelligent and a better worker.

There is no reference to specific dates in the history of the Rottweiler until the first Breed Standard, which was written in 1883 and published in 1901. It is probable that the large draft dogs of some one hundred and fifty years ago, stood as high as the Rottweiler of today, but with more daylight showing underneath. Their skulls had less width, with a longer, more pointed muzzle; while colour in general conformed with our present black and tan. The smaller working version followed the general conformation of the draft dogs, but allowed a wide variation in colour including a considerable amount of white. It is likely that the tan markings were already a feature of both sizes – irrespective of the base colour of the coat. From a genetic point of view, tan markings and their location are extremely dominant and appear in many breeds, even though their presence may be obscured by the base colour.

During the latter half of the last century, the Rottweiler began to be unemployed. Cattle were no longer driven on foot for long distances, and it was illegal to use a dog for draft work – they had been replaced by donkeys. By 1905 the town of Rottweil had only a single Rottweiler bitch living within its confines. However, the breed had lived and worked alongside people for many generations, and this had resulted in a dog with many attractions as a companion and house dog. Their fame spread beyond the narrow confines of their original home, and the two sizes undoubtedly merged – for there was no longer the need to have two specific types of working dog. The records do not tell us when this merger took place. It was probably a gradual process as breeders saw the benefits of combining the power and strength of the draft dogs with the intelligence and working ability of the smaller herding type.

Towards the end of the last century the role of the dog in society began to change. The need to keep a dog as a working animal whether it be to hunt, to herd and guard livestock, or as a draft animal, steadily declined. At the same time the dog found a place with man as a friend and house pet. Humans no longer demanded that a dog must earn his keep and were prepared to keep him solely for the pleasure that he brought. Ever adaptable to circumstances, the dog settled into his new role. At the same time, man began to take a new interest in the animal that had lived and worked at his side for thousands of years. Pure working ability was no longer the sole criterion. While breeders recognized the value of intelligence and the capability of carrying out various tasks, they also set out to preserve the physical appearance of their favourite breed. They therefore started to control breeding so that all aspects of the breed were maintained and gradually became cemented in their make-up. The aim was that specimens of the breed mated together, produced offspring that were, in every way, similar to themselves. As breeds or breed types became established, the next stage was to codify the desirable physical and mental characteristics of the selected breed and produce what we now call a Breed Standard. In virtually all breeds, the type had become established by the acid test of fitness for purpose, whatever it may have been. The Breed Standard set out to describe these characteristics on paper.

Today, man rightly believes that animals – both wild and domestic – should be preserved, irrespective of whether the animal serves any useful purpose. At the beginning of the century this attitude was less widely accepted, and the dog was lucky to be one of the first animals to receive this special attention. The aim was to preserve a chosen breed in its existing form and still capable of carrying out its original purpose. The fact that its physical characteristics were, in detail, of comparatively recent origin and that its purpose was in many cases no longer possible or even desirable, was conveniently ignored. Furthermore, the nature of man being what it is, he immediately set out to improve and refine the breed which had attracted him. The next logical step was his desire to breed a better dog than his neighbour and prove it, either by working it in some form of working test or by winning with it at a dog show.

The first Breed Standard for the Rottweiler was written in 1883, although not actually published until 1901. It was produced by the International Club for Leonberger and Rottweiler Dogs, and it has been suggested that the standard covered both breeds. Reading the 1901 Breed Standard and the current Leonberger Breed Standard, we find this difficult to believe, and prefer the explanation that the club, rather than the standard, covered both breeds in order to represent the major Swabian breeds.

The 1901 Breed Standard describes what we would recognize as a Rottweiler, but it is mainly of interest as a picture of the breed as it was at that time. It gives no measurements, merely describing the dog as medium to large. It does make the point that present-day standards ignore, although breeders have always accepted it, that bitches will be longer in the back. It is with regard to colour that the 1901 Breed Standard is most revealing. It states that the most common and preferable colour is black with russet or yellow markings, but it also accepts a number of alternatives for the base colour, although the tan markings are always demanded. The alternative base colours are: black stripes on an ash grey background, in other words, brindle; plain red; or dark wolf grey with black head and saddle. It also states that white markings on chest and legs frequently occur and are admissible if not too extensive. A stumpy tail is preferred and the Breed Standard implies that many dogs were born with a natural dock. A separate source gives the ideal height and weight of the Rottweiler in 1883 as about 23.5 inches and 66lbs. Measurements made during the First World War give heights around 24 inches for dogs and 21.5 inches for bitches. Weights are given as 54 to 61lbs. for dogs and 45 to 57lbs. for bitches. We are therefore looking at a dog that was a couple of inches shorter at the shoulder than their present-day counterparts, but only about half their weight.

The growing interest in dogs created the need for breed societies and for dog shows. Over the years the German breed clubs who took responsibility for the Rottweiler have, quite understandably, maintained a firm control over the breed, and the modern Rottweiler probably owes as much to these breed societies as to the actual breeders who implemented the club policy. This is in direct contrast to the situation in Britain and the U.S.A., where the fate of the breed is in the hands of the breeders, with little influence being exercised by the breed clubs. The effects, advantages and disadvantages of these two approaches will be discussed in more detail in Chapter Six, *The Rottweiler in the Community.*

The combined Leonberger and Rottweiler Breed Club had a short life, and in 1907 two clubs, acting exclusively for the Rottweiler, were formed. The first, the German Rottweiler Club, was founded in Heidelberg on January 13th. As frequently happens with breed clubs, a splinter group broke away and formed the South German Rottweiler Club in April 1907. The reason given for the split was "the expulsion of a member because of gross infringement of the principles of genuine sport". One can only surmise as to the details of this 'heinous' offence! The splinter group did not last long and was soon absorbed by a third club, the International Rottweiler Club. The SDRK left one interesting legacy. Its Breed Standard demanded a pincer bite. This requirement stems from the fact that, in the wild, predatory animals have a pincer bite. A number of experts have suggested that in demanding a scissor bite we are applying what is desirable in humans to our dogs. The dog, whose jaws are limited to an up or down movement, uses his molars to bite off pieces of food and his incisors for grooming himself, and for gnawing small pieces of flesh from bones. By insisting that the pincer bite is undesirable we are not only denying the dog the opportunity to do these things, but are also moving towards an excessively overshot bite which is not only unattractive but detrimental to the well-being of the dog.

The two clubs ran in parallel, and probably in opposition to each other until 1921. A Breed Standard issued in 1913 by the IRK continues to include variations in colour. The colours listed, apart from black and tan, are brown with yellow markings, blue, or plain red with black mask and black line running down the back. This last colour gives rise to speculation over the introduction, if any, of Mastiff or perhaps Boxer blood. This Breed Standard also lists white markings as a fault. The sizes given are slightly smaller than those required today, but not enough to be significant.

In 1910 an event took place which had a major effect on the Rottweiler. It was officially recognised in Germany as the fourth police dog breed. The other three were the German Shepherd Dog, the Doberman and the Airedale Terrier. The effect of this recognition was two-fold. Firstly, the Rottweiler had found a new role, one which has continued to the present day. Secondly, its use as a police dog meant that considerable emphasis was placed on developing those aspects of its character which were useful in this role.

In 1921 on August 14th, following a year of negotiation between the DRK and the IRK, the two clubs merged to form the General German Rottweiler Club (ADRK). From that date Germany had a single Rottweiler club controlling the breed and guiding its destiny. Today we have a Breed Standard which, with only minor exceptions of implementation rather than detail, is accepted worldwide. It is easy to forget that up to 1921, with a multiplicity of clubs, each with its own Breed Standard, there were quite wide variations in what was considered desirable for the breed. The ADRK set out to unify the breed under one controlling body, and to eliminate the variations in type which still existed. To those who believe that the Rottweiler as we know it today, has existed in this form for generations or even for centuries, it may come as a shock to realise that it was less than seventy years ago, in 1923, that the decision was made to eradicate colours other than black and tan. From that year onwards pedigrees were not granted to dogs of other colours. Equally revealing was the decision taken in 1924, that pedigrees would only be granted to dogs that were clearly pure-bred Rottweilers with both parents entered in the breed book.

Long-coated dogs were excluded from breeding, although anyone who knows the breed today will realise that this fault has not been entirely eliminated. This problem has been partly perpetuated by the failure of breeders to recognise a mild degree of 'long coatedness' when they see it. In fairness to the long-coated dog, they have also aided their own survival by their intelligence and gentle nature – qualities which seem to go with the long coat. The difficulty of eliminating the long coat and also the white markings, makes us wonder at the speed with which the other colours were eradicated. We think it fair to assume that these colours were only present to a very limited degree. Certainly there seems to be no photographic evidence of other colours, and early paintings associated with the Rottweiler only show the dog as black and tan.

From its formation, the ADRK has worked steadfastly to mould the breed in the form which it considered it should take. For over forty years the trend was towards the external appearance of the dog and, while its working qualities were never forgotten, there were those in the ADRK who were worried that an undue emphasis on appearance could be at the cost of the breed's working ability. As a result, strict controls were introduced on breeding stock, with temperament and working ability being taken into account – as well as physical appearance.

Although the ADRK, which has remained in control of the breed in Germany up to the present day, has placed great emphasis on the working ability of the Rottweiler, the fact remains that the dog has changed to a considerable degree during the last seventy to eighty years. The breed has become heavier, squarer in outline and with thicker bone. Heads have changed from the hound-like head of the hunting dog towards the mastiff type. A comparison of photographs of Leo von Cannstatt, considered to be one of the great early sires, in 1908 and Harras von Sofienbusch in 1963 – one of the greatest Rottweilers ever bred – shows two very different dogs. There is no doubt that the changes that have taken place have been aesthetic, with an eye on the show ring, rather than functional. Fortunately the Rottweiler's intelligence and character, acquired after generations of breeding for work, are deeply embodied in his ancestry. Changes in his physical appearance have not destroyed these assets, although blind pursuit of show success has, on occasion, produced stock of undesirable temperament, an aspect discussed in later chapters.

It is debatable whether the modern Rottweiler is fit for his original purpose. The dog of today is more akin to the heavy draft version than to the lighter cattle dog. Some experts have pointed out that the head size and shape, the hard bite and reduced agility would limit the dog's ability to work and drive cattle. Working enthusiasts have complained that the breed is too heavy for the jumps and scales used in trials, and its build can detract from the almost mechanical expertise required in obedience competition. At the same time, the Rottweiler's all-round ability, intelligence and enthusiasm for work have found many supporters. Police dog handlers who have taken the trouble to develop the dog's skills have found the Rottweiler to be an excellent dog for their purpose, even if a little too tough for civilian police work.

It has long been accepted that the Breed Standard describes the ideal dog to carry out a particular function or functions. The dog that conforms to the Breed Standard should be fit and able to carry out the purpose for which the breed was originally developed – fitness for purpose, even though the original purpose is no longer possible or even desirable. Breeds are often criticized for being unable to carry out the task for which they were intended. However, when applied to the Rottweiler, fitness for purpose is by no means clear-cut, and the definition of purpose becomes a problem when the original purposes covered three separate tasks – draft dog, cattle-herding dog and police dog – each task, to a certain extent, in conflict with the others. If you then bear in mind the additional complication that the first two tasks were carried out by two different types of dogs, then you will see that to relate the present-day Rottweiler and the Breed Standard to an original purpose becomes virtually impossible.

After looking at all the factors that have shaped the present day Rottweiler, we are forced to the conclusion that there is no clear single line of descent from the dogs that lived and worked in and around the town of Rottweil – they have changed as the world has changed. This is not a criticism of either the Rottweiler or of those who have shaped its destiny. It is, in fact, an acknowledgement of the qualities of the breed and of the excellence of the characteristics handed down by its many and varied forefathers.

What is more important is the breed's future. Fitness for purpose should be considered as fitness to fit into the community of today. It is essential for the survival, not only of the Rottweiler but of all breeds, that they are able to adapt themselves to the world in which they live. Any breed which fails to do so will only survive under restricted conditions under which the breed's qualities will soon be lost – a fate that the Rottweiler does not deserve. If the breed fails to adapt, then the fault will lie not with the dog but with those humans who, either from ignorance or design, have misused their responsibilities. The Rottweiler of today has retained the intelligence, courage, good nature, devotion, obedience and loyalty which was called for in the early standards, and this is still required today. The dog is still able to work livestock, and many do. Many have been trained to pull a cart, although we would not advocate that a dog spends its life working in this way. The breed has much to offer, working for man as a police dog, in tracking and rescue work and as a guard. It can be a faithful and devoted friend to its owner and family, and will be an ideal house pet and companion, if that is all that is required. If, as we hope you will, you ask more of your dog and want to compete in working trials, obedience competitions or the show ring, then a Rottweiler will do its utmost to please you. It may not be perfect for all these things, but it will compensate for this by its versatility. Although its physical appearance has changed from the early days, most will agree that this is for the better. The Rottweiler has been refined into a dog who can only be described as handsome. Its strong sturdy body and confident bearing make it a dog that catches the eye. Proof of this can be seen in the popularity it has achieved all over the world – a popularity which has regrettably brought disadvantages as well as advantages.

This then is the Rottweiler as it was, and as it is today. While it has achieved enormous success in the U.S.A., Britain and many other countries, the foundation of this success was laid in Germany by the German breed club and the dedicated breeders who worked with it. It does not detract from the work of the American, British and other breeders to say that we owe much to Germany for giving us the Rottweiler.

The Rottweiler is a good-natured and good-humoured dog. *Pearce.*

Chapter Two

THE CHARACTER OF THE ROTTWEILER

When a puppy is born, it can be likened to a blank sheet of paper, or, more accurately, a blank sheet of lined paper complete with margins. The lines and margins may be taken as the hereditary character or basic nature of the dog. They are already present and, while you may modify or write over these lines by training and environment, they will never disappear. What is written between these lines – the way the dog's character develops, and the way it behaves – is your responsibility and this is dealt with in subsequent chapters. In this chapter we are discussing the Rottweiler's basic nature – the character and abilities handed down to it by its parents and its ancestors.

   Although we are discussing temperament and behaviour, you must never lose sight of the fact that we are talking about a large powerful dog, weighing as much as a man, and probably better coordinated. The type of behaviour that may be acceptable or even attractive in a tiny Yorkshire Terrier is probably totally unacceptable in a

Rottweiler. This factor is also relevant when we discuss rearing and training.

In general, the hereditary qualities of the Rottweiler have been deliberately sought after, and in many instances they are listed in the Breed Standard as being desirable. However, some of these qualities, for example, courage, fearlessness and natural guarding instincts, are, as the Rottweiler has found to his cost, capable of being misused by man. The same characteristics in a man can, subject to training, motivation and environment, produce a hero or a criminal. With the dog, it is man who decides which way these characteristics are developed. If you find that your Rottweiler has developed in the wrong way, the fault is yours. You have either failed in your training and upbringing, or bred from stock that does not have the correct qualities. Lovers of the breed must also accept that there will always be people who, for reasons of their own, will deliberately misuse the Rottweiler's inherent qualities. Inevitably, there will be unaccountable blemishes on that virgin piece of paper – occasionally a dog will show a rogue temperament which is not typical of its breeding. You may argue that this type is a 'one off', and has no bearing on its heredity, but it is almost certainly due to some latent factor in the dog's ancestry. If you breed from such stock, you run the grave risk of perpetuating the fault in future generations.

No two dogs look exactly alike, even though they may both conform to the Breed Standard, and there is similar variation in individual characters. Some years ago an owner, whose much-loved Rottweiler had just died, came to us for a replacement. His requirement was quite simple. He wanted a dog exactly like the last one. We pointed out to him all dogs are different, and that he must not fault his new puppy because it was not the same as its predecessor – the puppy must be loved for its own character. In an attempt to explain this more clearly, we said: "It's like marrying a second wife – she will not be the same as the first. He replied: "No, thank God!" However, it proved our point.

The differences between the characters of individual dogs can also be shown by the varying approaches of stud dogs to their task. Virtually all Rottweilers are keen stud dogs. However, they achieve their aim in many different ways. Some will hurl themselves on the bitch with enormous enthusiasm but with little finesse, creating a problem of communication in every sense of the word. Others will adopt an attitude of stern domination, firmly telling the bitch to stand still and behave and enforcing their demand by a growl and a thump from a paw. A third approach, and we own an example at the moment, is the dog who will go to endless lengths to talk the bitch into it – rolling on his back and generally playing the clown; the bitch becomes so intrigued by his antics that she forgets any opposition and cooperates willingly.

In order to discuss the character of the Rottweiler, we will look at the various character requirements as laid down in the German, American and British Breed Standards, using the British Standard as our base because we played a considerable part in writing the first one, issued in 1965. The format and content of British Breed Standards is strictly controlled by the Kennel Club and they do not allow the detailed and valuable explanations and comments contained, for example, in the German Breed Standard. The German Standard is usually issued in conjunction with with a detailed commentary elaborating on various aspects of the Standard. As this is not an actual part of the FCI/ARDK Standard, the commentary is not included in the reproduction of the Breed Standard in Chapter Eight. However, in this chapter, some of the items quoted are from the commentary and will not be found in the Standard.

Before analysing the Rottweiler character in detail, it is worth looking at the national attitudes towards dogs in general and the guarding breeds in particular. In Germany the guarding breeds are accepted as being hard dogs who have a job to do – tough characters that you do not take liberties with. The dog is given respect and dignity. If you walk along the pavement with a Rottweiler or other guarding breed on a lead, the passers-by will walk round you. In Britain and elsewhere the dog is loved rather than respected. As a result, walking a guard breed in a public place means that the world, his wife and his child expect to be able to fuss over, handle and cuddle any dog they see. Unfortunately, when a dog occasionally reacts badly to this treatment, love turns to hate and the Press and the public turn violently against dogs, creating a small but vocal minority of anti-dog people. This situation is aggravated by the attitude of some British dog owners who believe that their dog can do no wrong and that it should be treated as an especially privileged creature – a sentiment which many of us would agree with, but not when it is to the detriment of others. This difference in national attitudes is important when one is studying the character of a breed and its ability to fit into the community.

It is extremely significant that the German Breed Standard and commentary devotes some four hundred words to the requirements of character and behaviour. The American Standard covers the subject in about one hundred words, excluding instructions on dealing with shyness and viciousness; and the British Standard considers twenty-eight words to be sufficient to list what is desirable in both character and temperament. Both the British and, to a lesser extent, the American Standard make it very clear that the main interest is in the physical appearance of the dog, primarily aimed at the show ring. We freely admit that, to a show-oriented world, the physical perfection of the dog is of major importance, and we also accept that almost all serious breeders pay at least some attention to character and temperament. However, the Rottweiler, like all breeds, has to live in the real world and the vast majority of them live in pet homes as part of the family. The character of the Rottweiler is far too important for the Breed Standard to dismiss it in a few words; it constitutes a disservice to both the dog and the community. We also accept that both the British and American Standards give a "potted guide" to the desirable Rottweiler character, but we consider it essential that the various aspects which make up the character and temperament of the Rottweiler should be included.

The first requirement of the Breed Standard as to character comes under the heading 'Characteristics', and it states that: "Appearance displays boldness and courage." The ideal Rottweiler does not merely appear to be bold and courageous. He is bold and courageous. The German Breed Standard, which includes a lengthy list of qualities, stipulates the degree required under under the divisions of 'high', 'medium' and 'low'. In this instance it asks that the dog's courage should be 'very high'. The behaviour of a dog who is required to be courageous does not, of course, stop with the mere use of the word. Courage also requires determination, confidence and will power. The sum of these qualities can, at times, manifest itself as a desire to dominate any person or anything which, in the Rottweiler's opinion, threatens its position of superiority. This determination to dominate creates one of the major problems between dog and master which have to be solved by any Rottweiler owner.

The determination to dominate manifests itself most clearly in the Rottweiler's attitude to other dogs and, in particular to other Rottweilers, but its intelligence and deep-rooted affinity with man means that it is willing to subordinate itself to its master, provided that the proper relationship is established at an early age. With regard to its attitude to other dogs, we have never felt that this is a fault, as long as it is properly controlled. A Rottweiler believes that it is superior to all other four-footed creatures – how else would it have been able to control cattle, animals many times larger than itself? The Rottweiler is confident of its own superiority, and will therefore co-exist peaceably with other dogs and other animals; it may even be protective towards them, so long as it is accepted that the Rottweiler is the superior being.

The various aspects of the Rottweiler character tend to merge and modify the effects of each other. The German Breed Standard points out that under threat the Rottweiler has a highly developed instinct to retaliate, and that it will not be deflected by pain or fear. Some years ago we had a typical example of the Rottweiler's courage combined with his ability to enjoy life as a member of a family. A friend worked for a security company, and his job was to ride in a separate vehicle behind the vehicle carrying cash. He travelled with a German Shepherd Dog trained for security work. At home he had a young Rottweiler male which he had bought when it was a puppy as a pet for his wife. The dog lived with the family, including their two young children, and enjoyed life as a house pet. The Shepherd died when the Rottweiler was about two years old, and our friend, who was a very knowledgeable dog trainer with years of experience in Rottweilers, decided to use his young male as a replacement. One day the cash truck was held up by raiders armed with shotguns. The Rottweiler was sent in to attack and took the full blast of a charge of shot which blew him across the pavement. In spite of his wounds the dog picked himself up and returned to the attack routing the raiders. As his owner said afterwards, the Rottweiler certainly saved the cash and almost certainly saved the owner from death or serious injury. The story had a happy ending. The dog recovered from his wounds and continued to work as a security dog, while also remaining as a much-loved family pet.

We all admire the courage and determination of the Rottweiler, and it would be a sad day if these characteristics were ever lost. However, as we said earlier, courage of this degree can be misused. In the hands of a criminal, or even a misguided or ignorant person, the Rottweiler can become a lethal weapon. The dog does not have an instinctive understanding of right or wrong as understood by humans. It can only follow its own instincts, which differ from ours, and the guidance given by its master.

The second characteristic in the Breed Standard is "self-assured and fearless". The German Standard asks that the Rottweiler's self-confidence should be high. The American modifies this by adding: "A self-assured aloofness that does not lend itself to immediate and indiscriminate friendships." Although we would agree that the Rottweiler does not immediately fawn on all and sundry, this requirement for aloofness would seem to be in disagreement with the German desire for a "basically friendly" nature. In our experience, the Rottweiler can be aloof and standoffish until properly introduced. As soon as the dog's master makes it clear that the stranger is a 'friend', it will immediately accept this evaluation. The Rottweiler is a confident dog; it is certain in its own mind that it is capable of dealing with any problem. It also has a strong sense of its own dignity and does not take kindly to being treated lightly.

The third characteristic asked for in the British Standard is: "A calm gaze should indicate good humour." This is virtually the same as the German requirement. Surprisingly, the American Standard does not call for this quality. The German Standard also asks for a "friendly and peaceable nature". Given the overall toughness of the breed, we consider that it is important that this quality, together with the requirement of "good nature" (under Temperament), should be emphasised as a very desirable modification of the dog's otherwise hard character. In our opinion, the Rottweiler is generally both good-natured and good-humoured. In fact, we would go so far as to say that he has a sense of humour. Anyone who has lived with a Rott will know that there are times when it will laugh with you and even laugh at you or tease you. Sadly, many Rottweilers today seem to have lost these qualities, either because they have been kept without the close contact with humans which they need, or because of deliberate emphasis on aggression by their owners. Such owners select breeding stock and design their training with the sole aim of producing an aggressive dog. Others ignore serious character faults in their search for physical perfection.

Under the heading of 'Temperament', the British Standard includes the word "biddable". The same term is used in the Boxer's Breed Standard. Strictly speaking, the dictionary definition of biddable is "docile; obedient". Many would argue that docile is not a word you would apply to the Rottweiler, although it is certainly capable of being extremely obedient. Those of us who played a part in formulating the British Breed Standard looked for a word which would convey the dog's intelligence and willingness to learn and work – requirements which are contained in both the German and American Standards. Regrettably, the breed's willingness to learn makes it easy for anyone to misapply the Rottweiler's qualities.

All three Breed Standards, in different ways, call for what is described in the British Standard as "natural guarding instincts". The instinct to guard its own territory, its own possessions and, above all, its owner, family and property is certainly very strong and is inherent in the breed. Many owners fail to realise that this instinctive willingness to guard is almost always present in the Rottweiler and, as a result, they over-stimulate the guarding instinct. We have sold many puppies to people who, while wanting a Rottweiler as a family pet, also wanted to benefit from its ability as a guard. Some merely encouraged the dog to guard on every possible occasion; others announced that they were sending the dog away for guard training. One media star associated with the police had even arranged for his Rottweiler to be trained at a police dog school. In every case we had to explain to the owner that the Rottweiler is a natural guard and that it would provide all the guarding that they would need, without any further encouragement. Any attempt to arouse the guarding instinct still further would mean that the dog would become too tough for normal domestic life and would be more than they could handle. Living with the family, the dog required control, training and encouragement to be friendly. The dog's love for its family would be sufficient incentive to protect them if necessary. Furthermore, the Rottweiler is able to sense from the tone of its master's voice, whether it is required to be a friend or a protector.

The British Breed Standard goes on to give negative requirements: "not nervous, aggressive or vicious". The German Standard makes similar demands, although it does not list aggression as a fault. It is reasonable to assume that the use of the word 'vicious' is considered to cover aggression, although it can also be argued that aggression in the sense of being willing to attack, if it is necessary, is desirable. One of the problems of translation is in finding the precise meaning and intention of the words used. The American Standard makes the excellent point that "an aggressive or belligerent attitude towards other dogs should not be faulted". Experienced Rottweiler owners and judges have always considered that the Rottweiler's pride, and certainty of its own superiority, coupled with its willingness to prove it, should not be considered a fault. This is an attitude which some non-specialist judges, accustomed to having their dogs presented to them as characterless 'wooden indians', would not agree with.

The British Kennel Club does not allow disqualifying faults in any of its Breed Standards. This means that a dog is never disqualified from competing in the show ring because of a fault in its appearance. The judge has to assess each dog against its Breed Standard, and any fault should be weighed against its virtues. The dog is therefore judged as a whole: an otherwise excellent specimen cannot be dismissed because of one fault, such as eye colour. As far as physical conformation is concerned, we would agree with this approach. However, with regard to temperament faults, we have come to the conclusion that the British should seriously consider making them a disqualifying fault.The American Standard issues a very clear instruction that a judge shall excuse any shy Rottweiler from the ring. It very sensibly does not leave the decision entirely to the judge, with all the inherent risks of opinion and bias. It lays down a very clear definition of shyness which is worth quoting in full. It states: "Shyness – a dog shall be judged fundamentally shy if, refusing to stand for examination, it shrinks away from the judge". Secondly it states: "A dog that in the opinion of the judge menaces or threatens him/her, or exhibits any sign that it may not be safely approached or examined by the judge in the normal manner, shall be excused from the ring. A dog that in the opinion of the judge attacks any person in the ring shall be disqualified."

It is interesting to note that these instructions, contained in the 1990 American Standard are considerably less tough than those in the 1986 version. We prefer the earlier Standard and consider that these stipulations were necessary for the good of the breed. Personally, as judges, we would wish to exercise a certain amount of discretion when applying these rules to young puppies. In our opinion, they are entitled to gentle handling during their first months in the show ring. However, we cannot over-emphasise the importance of good temperament in a breed like the Rottweiler. Failure to pay sufficient attention to character can do, and is doing, untold harm to the breed and its reputation.

There are a number of aspects which are only covered in detail in the German Standard, although some of them may be implied, or taken as understood by American or British breeders. The Germans emphasise the Rottweiler's "strong attachment to its house and homestead". Certainly its devotion and love for its human family is one of the Rottweiler's most endearing traits. The Germans also state that it is fond of children. This picture of a dog acting as a faithful, loving and protective member of the family is true, as anyone who has owned a well trained and well balanced Rott will confirm. However, it is a statement that would be disputed by members of the public reading the popular Press during the last year or so, and it does need some qualification. Firstly, the Rottweiler is a big, powerful, and at times, boisterous dog. It can, quite unwittingly, injure or frighten a small child, even though its intention may only be to play with the child as it would with another dog. It needs to be taught that the child is something to be treasured and is not merely a toy for its amusement. We should also face facts and understand that a child's screams and cries can, in a dog of any breed, trigger the basic instinct that a dog has to attack an injured animal. This instinct goes back far beyond man's domestication of the dog, and it is inherent in an animal that, in the wild, found much of its food from the injured and the sick. Fortunately, man's development of the dog has overlaid this instinct to a great extent – but it is still there.

Love can generate jealousy, and the arrival of a new baby in the household, perhaps taking love and affection from the Rottweiler who has been there for several years, can cause problems. Quite often the situation is reversed and the Rott becomes extremely protective of the new arrival and decides to guard it against the enthusiastic attention paid to it by visitors and relations. As a result, grandfather complains that the dog is dangerous and the poor Rottweiler is banned to the kitchen or even thrown out altogether – a classic example of the dog doing what it thought was right, and suffering as a result. We would reiterate that the Rottweiler is good with children, but only if it has the true Rottweiler nature, and if the situation is treated with care and understanding. Certainly, no young child should be left alone with any dog until it has been clearly established that the child is to be treated gently and with affection and, in the case of older children, that the child understands that the dog is to be treated with respect. We would confidently claim that far more children have been saved from harm and even death, at the hands of humans, because the family Rottweiler was there to protect them, than have ever suffered injury from one.

The German Standard requires that the Rottweiler should have a "good capacity for tracking". Police handlers who have trained Rottweilers have always commented on their tracking ability and usually claim that, when a difficult track is required, the call goes out to bring on the Rott. We have found them to be natural trackers even without formal training.

The German Standard lists various qualities, and the degree expected for each trait. They are:

> Fearlessness: high.
> Stamina: high.
> Mobility and activity: medium.
> Mistrust: low/medium.
> Sharpness: low/medium.
> Hardness: high.
> Retrieving: medium/high.
> Threshold of excitability: medium/high.
> Searching instinct: medium.

In general, the list is self-explanatory, and we have already discussed most of the traits. The demand for high stamina has to be considered in relation to the dog's size and weight, and it is almost certainly not as high as that of his cattle-driving ancestors. We have always been a little worried about the term "sharpness", which in the English-speaking world tends to be used in a slightly derogatory manner, implying snappiness. However, if it implies a quick reaction, it makes more sense. In any case, it is only rated as "low/medium". The requirement that the threshold of excitability should be "medium/high" must not be misread. The demand is that the dog should not easily become excited. In other words, he should be reasonably calm and controlled.

The disqualifying temperament faults in the German Standard are of interest as an illustration of their determination to ensure that the character of the Rottweiler is maintained. Dogs who fail in the following ways cannot be used for breeding and must be disqualified: "timid, cowardly, shy, gun-shy, vicious, excessively mistrustful and nervous".

Other countries may not wish to adopt the mandatory approach used by the Germans, but breeders would be well advised to apply such constraints to their own breeding programmes. There are some Rottweilers being bred from who fail in these ways – admittedly a minority – and as a result not all Rottweilers are worthy representatives of the breed.

Much has always been made of the Rottweiler's origin as a herding dog, so it is therefore surprising that, apart from some physical characteristics which reflect such work, none of the Breed Standards make an attempt to list any of the qualities required of such a dog, and they do not even mention its herding past. This is in contrast to the British Breed Standard for the German Shepherd Dog, which is described as a "versatile working dog", and for the Rottweiler's close relation, the Bernese Mountain Dog, which is described as a "multi-purpose farm dog". The British Standard for the Rottweiler makes no mention of work. The American and German Standards mention willingness to work and emphasise that it is a working dog, without stating the type of work involved. The Rottweiler's versatility is integral to the breed. This is a trait it has shown from its origins as a cattle herd and draft dog to its approval and success as a police dog. We must conclude that the aim of those who have guided the Rottweiler for the last hundred years has been to produce a dog capable of working as an extremely able police dog and, even more commendably, as a devoted house dog able to love and protect its human family. All else is in the past and no longer relevant. The Rottweiler has now carved out an important and useful role for itself which suits the demands of modern life – quite an achievement for a dog that started life trudging along a dusty road behind a herd of cattle.

However, ownership of a Rottweiler should not be undertaken lightly. This dog is not only intelligent, it is also determined and even wilful. It is powerful and capable of doing serious injury if its capabilities are misused or not properly controlled. To own or breed Rottweilers carries great responsibility. Any lover of the breed must do all in their power to ensure that these dogs do not fall into the wrong hands, and that the correct character and temperament are preserved. This is not a dog for those who are mentally or physically incapable of training and controlling it. The Rottweiler has achieved enormous popularity in many countries, and this has proved to be a mixed blessing. The dog has become a commercial success, and this has inevitably resulted in the wrong people breeding the wrong dogs for the wrong reasons. If the Rottweiler is to have the future that it deserves, then that future lies in fewer dogs – and those in the hands of people who understand them and love them, and who will work to protect their future.

Chapter Three

PUPPY TRAINING

If you decide to own a Rottweiler you must accept that you have a great responsibility to the dog, to yourself and your family, and to the community. In this chapter we will look at the methods of raising and training your Rottweiler; we are not going to discuss which type of biscuit to feed or what bedding to use – important though they are – but we want to concentrate on the vital mental conditioning that you instil in your dog. A fit and healthy animal is essential, but even more important is that it is mentally balanced and properly controlled. We have used the phrase 'raising and training', but in reality we are dealing with character development. The Rottweiler has a great deal of character, all of it can be good if it is properly developed, but if it is not channelled in the right direction, bad traits will soon emerge.

We are going to assume that your Rottweiler is primarily one that will live in the house, be a friend to you, your family, your relations and those visitors you welcome to your home. It should be obedient without being servile; it should be a happy dog who enjoys the life it leads with you, without any of the psychological hang-ups which make it bite without good cause, bark whenever it is left alone, or chew up the furniture. In addition, we hope that your Rottweiler will be protective towards you and yours, while retaining the ability to differentiate between the butcher and the burglar. You may also wish to take part in other activities with your dog: exhibiting at dog shows, competing in obedience, or working trials or agility competitions, or even real work such as security work or as a farm dog herding stock. If you do use your Rottweiler for any of these hobbies or tasks, we hope that it will still be first and foremost a friend and companion.

Our own involvement with the Rottweiler has been primarily in the show world but, proud as we have been of our Show Champions, the dogs that have given us the greatest pleasure are those that we have competed with in obedience and in working trials. There is enormous satisfaction and happiness to be gained when you and your dog, working and training together, achieve a successful result. There is no doubt that the most satisfying relationship between dog and man is that consisting of one dog and his owner forging a close bond with each other. In the show world, a successful career for a dog probably lasts about three years. After that, it is a question of bringing out another youngster and giving the old dog a happy retirement for the rest of its life. Conscientious show kennels rapidly acquire a lot of pensioners, some of which they may be able to find excellent pet homes for, and others which they may keep themselves. Breeders with less conscience will have these dogs put down or sell them, regardless of the purchaser's suitability, or even send them overseas, getting a better price than they would have fetched at home. A dog that competes in obedience or working trials can carry on for as long as its legs will carry it. The show dog will lose some of its beauty as it grows old, but the working dog will get better at its task as it grows older.

The Rottweiler is a strong, powerful dog, and it has a strength of character to match. Inevitably, it attracts those who want to own such a dog for the wrong reasons. At the worst extreme, the Rottweiler is required as protection for criminal activities. In this instance, all we can do is hope that the dog does not suffer because of your wrong-doing. More commonly, the Rottweiler is seen as an appendage for those people who wish to project a macho image but only have the personality of a rabbit. They fondly imagine that a big, powerful dog will compensate for their own weakness: in fact, body building or a course in martial arts would be of more use to them. Owning a Rottweiler is not the answer and can never compensate for lack of strength of character in the human. Even if you plead not guilty to the above charges, you may still not be the ideal Rottweiler owner. This is a breed with a strong, dominant temperament, and if you are not capable of dominating a Rottweiler mentally, then it will dominate you. Physical strength and brute force will not solve the problem. In any trial of physical strength, there is a strong possibility that the dog will win, possibly with disastrous results. On the other hand, if you succeed in breaking the dog physically, you will have an animal that only obeys through fear – its confidence and trust have been destroyed. This type of dog, known as a 'fear-biter' by the Germans, is a travesty of the Rottweiler as described in the Breed Standard.

One of our few failures in finding the right type of home for a Rottweiler involved a friend who was an extremely kind and gentle person. His wife and children had a similar approach to life, and nobody in the household ever raised their voice or lost their temper. Everything was done by calm, pleasant persuasion, and at no time did anyone say "You will do this or else!" As a result, the young male puppy very quickly decided that if no one else was going to be boss, he would be. By the time the dog was eighteen months of age he would not do anything unless it suited him. Fortunately the dog retained his excellent nature, and as no one ever tried to force the issue, there was no confrontation. On the day that they finally brought him back to us, it had taken half an hour to persuade him to get into their car, although he obeyed instantly, albeit with a look of some surprise, when one of us told him firmly to shut up and get in. The story ended happily. We exchanged him for a Labrador puppy whose character fitted in perfectly with the family, and the Rottweiler went to a home that understood the Rottweiler temperament.

One of the early Rottweiler pioneers in England was a small woman who certainly weighed a lot less than the Rottweilers she owned and trained very successfully. She was, however, a very strong personality and none of her Rottweilers ever dared to step out of line. Neither, in fact, did many humans! Her large and very tough Rottweilers, one of whom became a working trials Champion, were controlled solely by force of personality. Physical strength did not come into it. Her Rottweilers used to ride in the back of her estate car, normally sitting up so that they could watch the world go by. However, the moment she put the car into reverse gear, without a single command, three large dogs would immediately lie flat on the floor and remain there until the manoeuvre was completed. All her dogs gave instant obedience to their owner, but they also gave her their love and respect. This small but determined lady also expected that other humans should be able to exert the same control and will power that she possessed. On one occasion we were practising the 'send away' – training a dog to move out in front in a straight line and stop on command at a selected spot. Luther, our Dutch import, a dog with a strong sense of his own dignity and an independent turn of mind, got halfway and then decided to cock his leg. Like many Rottweilers, Luther always performed this function while giving anyone in the vicinity a cold stare, which made it clear that he did not expect to be interrupted. The small lady turned to us and said: "Don't let him do that." Luther was thirty yards away and not on a lead. We both looked rather helpless and said: "Well, how do we stop him?" "Just don't allow it," said the small lady. By this time, Luther had finished and condescended to complete his send away. While we are sure that her own dogs would never have dared to offend in this way, we personally have never managed to achieve quite such complete domination.

The key to the successful upbringing of your Rottweiler is a combination of firmness, fairness and mutual respect. Your aim must be to achieve mental domination so that your dog wants to please you and is unhappy if he fails you. Nice, normal, balanced people, produce nice, normal, balanced dogs: only if you can qualify in this way should you own a Rottweiler. The experts tell us that only some twenty per cent of a dog's character is acquired by training. The remaining eighty per cent is instinctive, inherited from its wild ancestors. A figure of thirty per cent is credited to inheritance from tamed forebears, who also carry the instincts of their wild ancestors. While we are not very keen to try and reduce dogs to a mathematical formula, it is probably correct to say that half of your dog's character comes from his wild ancestors and half from his domestication by man. However, the many thousands of years of domestication have, in our opinion, modified many of the wild dog's instinctive reactions to a major extent, so that the majority of dogs show behaviour characteristics which are much more acceptable to man.

We live in the country, and we often suffer from an invasion of mice. At one time our two house dogs were a Jack Russell Terrier bitch and a young Rottweiler bitch. Fizz, the Jack Russell, would happily catch and kill the mice. Ophelia, the Rott, who had been taught that she must accept all the various forms of life in our household, eventually decided that catching mice appeared to be fun. However, killing them was beyond her gentle nature. We would find her in our kitchen, lying on the floor, with a live and very frightened, but quite unhurt mouse encircled by her paws. Occasionally, she would tenderly take the mouse in her mouth and then release it still unharmed, although she used her paws to rake it back to her when it tried to escape. When she eventually became bored with this game, she would allow the mouse, by this time on the verge of a nervous breakdown, to scuttle back to its hole by the door. On some occasions Fizz would lose her patience, take the mouse away from Ophelia and give it a compassionate coup de grace. Contrary to ill-informed opinion, the Rottweiler is a kind and gentle dog, and you must bear this sensitivity in mind from the beginning of your training.

The training and development of the character of your Rottweiler starts from the moment that it is born. If you buy a young puppy then you must hope, and in fact ensure, that the breeder makes the same effort to give it the same start in life as you would. We say breeder, because your puppy will certainly have the wrong start in life if you buy it from a dealer, a pet shop or some other third party. The Code of Ethics, issued by breed clubs in the U.S.A. and Britain, almost invariably demands that their members do not sell their puppies to such people. This rule is for the very good reason that a puppy bought from this source will have suffered the trauma of being transported, experiencing strange surroundings and being exposed to infection, change of diet and a lack of love and affection at a very crucial stage of its life. You will also be denied the opportunity of checking that its parents are the type of dog that you would wish to take into your home, and you will miss out on the after-sales back-up that a reputable breeder will give.

What happens to a puppy between three and twelve weeks can make an enormous difference to how it develops as an adult. If you are breeding a litter, the ideal place for your puppy to be born is in a room in your house; not a busy room with people passing through all the time, but a quiet room where it is easy for you to keep an eye on the bitch and her family. A utility room opening off the kitchen is ideal. The room should be warm, with provision for extra heating and for a properly constructed whelping box. It should also be comfortable enough for you to spend a considerable amount of time in there. Many people have their bitches whelp in their bedrooms – an excellent idea if the rest of the family do not object. Others reverse the procedure and move their bed into the whelping room during the crucial few days before and after the puppies are due. A Rottweiler bitch who has grown up with you will look to you for help and affection when her litter is born, so make it as easy as possible to be present. Some breeds that we have owned would refuse to produce their puppies when we were present. They would sit and stare at us, willing us to leave them alone. Eventually we have shut the door and left them to get on with it. When we have returned a couple of hours later they would have produced their puppies, cleaned everything up, and be lying quietly surrounded by their babies. Not so our Rottweilers – they almost always wanted 'Mum' to be around. The bitch who produced Champion Chesara Dark Charles always lived in the house. She slept in the hall and, although the door was always open, she would never come into our bedroom during the night. A few nights before she was due to whelp we were awakened by a cold nose and a scratching paw. We put her in the whelping room, next to the kitchen, left the door open and went back to bed. An hour later the same thing happened. This time we stayed with her, and secure in the knowledge that we were there to figuratively hold her hand, or more accurately, her paw, she settled down to produce her babies.

From the moment they are born, we handle our Rottweiler puppies. They are picked up to check that their tummies are full, that their bottoms are clean and that in general they are making satisfactory progress. Above all, they are handled so that they are used to the scent, sound and touch of humans. On the subject of sound and scent, if the chief midwife is a woman, then you must make sure that male voices are also heard by your puppies and vice versa. Puppies which have only heard female voices may show signs of fear at their first sound of a deep male voice. Contact with humans is vital, but this does not mean that the mother and her puppies should be disturbed by a stream of visitors during the first few days after they are born. At this stage visitors should be limited to those she knows and trusts.

It is not always possible to whelp a litter in the house, and so it may be necessary to use an outside whelping kennel. If this is the case, it is vital to keep up the same level of human contact; it simply means that you will just have to work harder and spend more time walking backwards and forwards between house and kennel. Many of the excuses for not having your bitch whelp in the house are just excuses, and nothing more. We once whelped and raised a litter in an upstairs bedroom of a Royal Air Force married quarter. We took all the furniture out and covered the whole floor with a large plastic tarpaulin, big enough to reach a couple of feet up the walls. It worked perfectly. If you are not willing to put yourself out so that your litter can have the best possible start in life, then you really should not be breeding Rottweilers. It is vital for the development of this breed that it should have close contact, familiarity, affection, and respect for humans, from the beginning of its life. Far too often breeders produce litters that have been shut away in a kennel with no human contact other than the one person looking after them and no unusual sights and sounds until at the age of eight weeks they are suddenly launched into the the wide and very frightening world. No wonder that they then show temperament problems. Breeders who fail in this way will sometimes argue that they have been intent on preventing any risk of infection. Of course you have to guard against infection, and you should take all reasonable precautions to ensure that the puppies are not put at risk. However, the best immunity is the natural one acquired by meeting a low level of infection. The puppy reared in totally sterile conditions is the one most likely to succumb when it subsequently meets infection after it is sold and goes out into the world. In any case, what is the point of rearing a puppy who is free from infection but who is a nervous wreck? Breeders who fail to socialise their puppies properly usually do so because they are ignorant, lazy or so busy turning out puppies for sale that they have neither the time nor the inclination to do the job properly.

If you are whelping a litter in the house, you can leave the door of the whelping room open after a few days so that the puppies can become accustomed to all the usual domestic noises – the washing machine, the vacuum cleaner, the sound of human voices, including children and strangers. It will be helpful if the door into the whelping room is of the stable type so that the bottom half can be kept closed to prevent the bitch from leaving her family in order to join you in the kitchen, especially if there is food around. The half-door also makes it easy to indulge in the delightful but time-consuming habit of puppy watching. Incidentally, we said that the whelping room should be quiet, and it may appear that we are now encouraging litters to be reared in a pandemonium of noise. However, there is a good reason why the room should not be located at the hub of the household's activity. If the room was close to the front door, for instance, you would probably find that every time the door bell rang, the bitch would jump from her box with protective roars, scattering puppies in all directions. If she does this, her strong claws could injure or even kill a puppy a few days old. Rottweilers are good mothers, but they can also be clumsy. The ideal whelping room is one that is close to you and your family, but it is protected from unexpected noise and interference which is outside your control.

By the time your puppies are three to four weeks old they should be accustomed to being picked up and handled, they should be used to hearing strange noises, and to being visited by people outside the immediate family. We encourage visitors to come and "talk to the puppies". The next door neighbour's children are useful in this capacity, although you must be sure that your bitch accepts them, or that she is put outside before you take the children in. This does not mean that your puppies should become a playground for the neighbourhood; neither does it mean that you should allow children to handle the puppies unless you are sure that they will not drop them, tread on them or experiment to see whether their heads will unscrew! We always ask children to sit down when they are playing with puppies. You must never miss an opportunity to talk to the puppies yourself. It is all too easy, when you are busy, to dash into the whelping room, put down a dish of food or do whatever it is that you wish to do, and go out again, all in complete silence. Husbands, wives and whoever else visits the puppies, must be trained to produce a flow of baby talk every time they go through the door.

From the age of about four weeks the puppies need to be able to explore beyond the immediate confines of the whelping box. Firstly they should allowed into an attached pen, and then gradually, as their confidence builds up, they can go further afield into a wider area such as your back garden. If your garden is an ornamental one, then you may have to choose between your roses and your Rottweilers. We allowed part of the garden outside the back door to become a sort of puppy adventure playground, full of holes, with space to dig more, old cardboard boxes which are popular for games of hide and seek, low wooden platforms for playing "I'm the king of the castle", and various assorted rubbish which became puppy

Rottweiler puppies should be sturdy self-assured characters; confident and friendly with humans.

treasures. Here our puppies could play and develop their confidence, while remaining under a watchful eye from the kitchen window. By the time that your puppies are about seven to eight weeks old they should be sturdy self-assured little characters, confident and friendly with humans and beginning to learn from you, their mother and their littermates the requirements of living with people and other animals. Obviously the world outside your back garden is still a large, frightening and dangerous place and a puppy's introduction to it must be gradual and it must be carefully supervised. However, if you have done everything right up to now, you should not have any problems.

As a general rule we like our puppies to go to their new homes at about seven and a half weeks of age. The next few weeks are the formative ones in a puppy's life, and the sooner they learn the ways of their new home, the better it will be. They should be fully weaned by about six weeks. By this time their mother will probably make it very clear that the joys of motherhood are wearing a bit thin and that it is time that she returned to her normal life. While you may feel that it is your duty and probably your pleasure to keep your puppies for several more weeks, you would not be doing them any favours. Once the pups are weaned, provided that they are strong and healthy, they are far better imprinting on their new home and owner than

Children should be encouraged to handle puppies.   *Times Newspapers Limited*

learning street gang behaviour with their brothers and sisters. A litter of Rottweilers run on together up to the age of twelve weeks or more will turn into an undisciplined mob and the problems of training each one as an individual will be far greater.

From now on we are going to assume that you are training a single puppy from about the age of eight weeks. Many people like to rear a pair of puppies together, and there is no reason why not. They will give each other confidence and you will enjoy hours of watching their puppy games. They will also lead each other into mischief and your job will be that much harder. If this is your first Rottweiler, we would suggest that one is quite enough to start with, and you will develop a closer bond with your dog if each of you gives the other your undivided attention.

If you have not bred your own puppy, its first journey will probably be in your car when you collect it from the breeder. We suggest that you take a passenger with you and that the puppy rides on the passenger's lap – suitably protected against accidents by an old towel. There are several reasons for this. Firstly, we have found that a puppy is less likely to be car-sick if it has the warmth and comfort of a human to snuggle against for its first few journeys. Secondly, the passenger can control it; puppies have a habit of crawling under the driver's feet if left loose in a car. Thirdly, some unthinking owners put the new puppy in a cage in the back, or even in the car boot. How would you feel if your first flight in an aircraft was spent in the baggage hold? Remember, the puppy is leaving home and is being separated from its littermates and all that is familiar. This can be a traumatic experience and it should be treated with kindness and patience.

There is one prime rule in training your puppy. Never allow the puppy to do anything which you would not wish it to do when it is an adult. What may be amusing and harmless behaviour by a ten-week-old baby Rottweiler can be annoying and even dangerous when the same thing is done by a fully grown adult. It is asking too much of the Rottweiler, intelligent though it is, that behaviour that was allowed and even encouraged in puppyhood, is suddenly unacceptable now that it is fully grown. What you are prepared to allow must be your decision. What may be perfectly admissible in a five-pound Yorkshire Terrier is probably quite unacceptable in a one-hundred-pound Rottweiler. Some of us will accept behaviour in our dogs which would be strongly disapproved of by others. For example, we allow our dogs to jump up at us in greeting or to show affection. We believe that when a fully grown male puts his paws on our shoulders while standing on his hind legs for a cuddle, we are exchanging the affection which we feel for each other. This is by no means the same thing as the dog standing over us growling in an attempt to show his dominance, although the animal behaviour 'experts' who are constantly producing pseudo-scientific theories about a dog's behaviour, seem to be unable to tell the difference. Our dogs are taught to get down when they are told and to understand that the cuddle is over. Some of these animal behaviour consultants – or animal psychologists as they like to be styled – frequently issue lists of things that your dog should not do. We are told that the dog should not sleep on the bed, it should not be allowed to sit longingly at one's elbow at meal times in the hope of a titbit, it should always eat food that is inferior to its master's, it should not be allowed to assume a position that is physically higher than yours such as the back of your chair, and it should not be allowed to give a clear indication by a shove with a wet nose that it would like its ears rubbed. The list is endless. Frankly, if our dogs did not do almost all these things they would not give us all the pleasure that they do. We have had Rottweilers that sleep on the bed. Whether you choose to allow this is up to you; to a certain extent it depends on the size of your bed and who else you share it with. There are, however, certain things that you should never allow your Rottweiler to do, mainly because of his character and physical strength. We will deal with these later. At this stage the important thing is to decide what you and your family will find acceptable. When making these decisions, you must bear in mind that what the male in the household may find amusing might not be popular with his wife and children.

Most trainers and text books will tell you that training should not begin before the age of six months. The majority of training classes will not accept dogs before this age. While this may be correct for formal training such as "sit", "down", the retrieve and high-quality heel work, all other aspects of training are the result of association and familiarisation, and this should commence virtually from birth. From the age of eight weeks the puppy should begin to learn what constitutes acceptable behaviour, and what is unacceptable. The first lesson we teach is a response to the use of the puppy's name. At this stage we do not expect an immediate rush to sit at our feet, but we do expect a reaction, which we will usually encourage by bribery. In our opinion, bribery is an acceptable ploy to use with a Rottweiler throughout its life. It is effective because the Rottweiler is greedy and susceptible to the offer of a tasty morsel of food, and we also consider it reasonable that virtue should bring a tangible reward. You should bear in mind that your puppy has probably already learnt that the collective call of "puppies" or "babies" signals the arrival of the food dish. Now it has to learn to associate its name with the same pleasure. The second requirement which we ask for at a very early age is a response to the word "No". In our household this means quite simply: "Whatever you are doing, stop it." It can be used to stop the puppy chewing the legs off the table, spending a penny on the carpet, or biting your ankle. The third basic order is "wait". This instruction solves some of the problems of a Rottweiler that is determined to go through every door the moment it is opened, irrespective of whether you wish it to do so or not. These three initial items of training go a long way towards establishing a happy relationship between you and your dog.

Life should be fun for your puppy at this stage. Its relationship with you should be cheerful, involving games and shared pleasures. The dog must learn that retribution follows wrong-doing, but you must refrain from constant nagging and punishment. We have emphasised that physical punishment does not work with Rottweilers. The exception is with the young puppy who has not yet learnt that there are good reasons for the code of behaviour that you demand. Even then, the physical punishment should be nothing more than a quick tap with one finger on the nose accompanied by a sharp "No". Contrary to some opinions, we have never found that a tap on the nose makes a puppy hand-shy; it is certainly far more effective than a smack on the bottom which merely provokes a casual glance to see what has happened. A bitch corrects her puppies when one of them nips her too hard, by a growl and a snap. The puppy is not injured in any way, but it soon realises that mother is cross and that it does not pay to misbehave. The ability to produce a growl of annoyance and a stern reprimand, even when you are not really annoyed, is part of the skill of puppy-training. Immediate and firm verbal condemnation of something that you do not approve of is your most effective weapon.

Punishment plays a very small part in successful training. Encouragement, on the other hand, is the key to almost all learning. Even when you have reprimanded your puppy for a misdeed, you should immediately restore its confidence by a kind word and a caress. It is pointless to nag and scold long after the dog has forgotten the reason for it. At all stages of training, retribution must be at the moment the offence is committed. You may feel angry for some time after your puppy has chewed up your slippers; but it has forgotten its misdeed, and is merely puzzled and distressed that you are still making a fuss. Substitution can be a very useful method of correction. Your puppy will consider that the 'treasure' it has just found – whether it is one of your best socks or the smelly corpse of a dead bird that it has found in the garden – is its own personal property, and any attempt to snatch it away will be resented. Ideally, you will have taught the command "leave", which means that you want whatever the dog has in its possession, and you expect to get it. However, in the early stages of training you will probably find that is much easier to offer an alternative – the puppy's favourite toy or a biscuit. Confrontation is something to be avoided with a Rottweiler; it is counter-productive and you are not being cowardly or a bad trainer if you try and find other methods.

A young Rottweiler will find that there are many strange and frightening sounds and objects in the home and outside. Its first reaction to the roaring monster that you call a washing machine will probably be to run away and hide, and possibly to bark at it from a distance. Do not try to force the dog to go up to the machine, pulling it by the collar. Let it take its own time. Unless the puppy is temperamentally unsound, it will gradually approach and investigate, while you make encouraging and reassuring noises. Confidence must be built up slowly; attempts to force the issue will probably result in a dog that is permanently nervous.

Your puppy should wear a little collar from about the age of seven weeks. Many breeders put collars on earlier as an aid to identification. Do not rush out and buy one that is expensive and elaborate at this stage, the puppy will grow out of it very rapidly. To begin with, your puppy may claim that it is totally crippled and unable to walk while wearing this thing around its neck, but it will soon get used to it. The next stage is to attach a very light lead to the collar and allow the puppy to take you for a walk. Do not attempt to make it follow you; the pulling at its neck will result in panic, and collars and leads will become unpleasant things in its mind. Just hold the lead loosely and allow the puppy to go where it wishes. It will gradually become accustomed to this link between you and accept that it is to go with you, rather than the reverse. Early lead training is an occasion for a lot of baby talk and encouragement. Even though you may be very proud of the way that your puppy walks on the lead, you should not show off by forcing it to take long walks to the shops on hard pavements. Start off by short walks around the garden, progressing by gradual stages to walks along the street. Remember that traffic and street noises will be a new experience, and may be a cause of alarm until the puppy gets used to it.

Most family dogs will be required to travel, and car sickness can be a problem. If your puppy is sick every time, then it will soon learn to hate the car; a journey with your family, which should be a pleasure, becomes a misery. From the age of seven or eight weeks all our puppies are taken for daily car rides sitting on the passenger's lap. At first the journey is only a few hundred yards, gradually increasing to longer trips. The best way to prevent the puppy being sick is to distract it by talking to it. It is not unusual to see one of us driving along the road reciting nursery rhymes or singing songs. We have not taken leave of our senses, we are just trying to prevent a puppy from being sick! Even when the puppy has outgrown the passenger's lap and has moved to the back of the car, we still carry on talking and distracting it, until it is ready to settle down happily.

Most dog people choose a motor car on the basis of its suitability as dog-transport, but many dog owners have other priorities governing their choice. However, you should give some thought as to how your particular vehicle can best be adapted. Once the dog has got past the baby puppy stage, it is probably best if it travels in a proper fitted dog cage in the back. Cages have lots of advantages: the dog is secure and cannot escape when the car doors are opened, it is protected from being thrown around in the car by braking and cornering, and, within reason, it can be left safely in the car with the tail gate and windows open when the car is parked. Cages can be bought to fit virtually any type of vehicle, and you can get cages with central divisions and access by rear and side doors. The ideal vehicle for your dog is an estate wagon, preferably with split rear doors hinged at the side. Most estate wagons have top-hinged doors, which means that if you do not have a dog cage, the door will hit you under the chin as the dog tries to push its way out before you can get it under control. This situation is one that calls for the use of the command "wait", which we mentioned earlier. Training to comply with this command may have to be enforced by a second person inside the car until the dog has learnt to obey.

Many owners have trouble persuading their dog to get in the car. You sometimes see a fully grown Rottweiler standing at the tail gate expecting to be lifted in - not an easy task. Trips in the car should be a pleasure to your dog. Many of our dogs are so keen to go for a drive that a visiting car left in the driveway with a door open will be full of dogs, much to the surprise of visitors! Some owners believe that a puppy will damage its legs scrambling into a car or jumping out. To prevent this they lift the dog in and out, and it becomes a habit. Obviously you must use common sense, but as soon as possible your Rottweiler should be encouraged to jump in and out on command. Try throwing in a biscuit or its favourite toy to encourage it. We had one bitch who would jump in and out via an opened front window, but perhaps this is not to be encouraged. If your car is a hatchback with a high sill to the rear door, it is probably better to use a side door as the normal entrance, at least until the dog is big enough to jump over the rear sill.

A cage, used indoors, is a useful aid to training. It must be of the weldmesh type so that the dog can see and hear what is going on around him. A solid crate, so that the dog is shut in the dark and out of contact with his surroundings will not do. The cage should not be used as a lazy man's easy way out. It should only be used on those occasions when it is essential that the puppy is kept under control – if you have to go out for a short time, at night, or if it is essential that the puppy is kept out of the way. The cage should be placed in a busy part of the house so that your puppy can continue to be aware of the everyday sights and sounds.

The first few months of a Rottweiler's life are the formative period. This is the time when the character of the adult dog is established – for better or for worse. Likes and dislikes, fears and pleasures learned in these months will carry on into adult life. Probably the first unpleasant experience that the puppy will have to suffer is its first visit to the veterinary surgeon for its protective inoculations. Rottweilers have long memories and the man in the white coat will be a lifelong bogeyman if this first visit goes badly. Some vets are not good at needlework, others can slip the needle in without arousing a murmur. Any new vet joining the practice that we use is intimidated by us demanding that he should not make the puppy cry. Failure will bring the senior partner on the scene, in case there should be a risk of losing a good customer. At least this means that he will be as gentle as possible. We have a firm rule that we are always present during veterinary treatment, and this certainly applies on the puppy's first visit. Some vets will try and insist that they take the puppy away from you to another room for treatment. Even if you are squeamish about such things, you owe it to your puppy to be present, giving it assurance and support. If the vet is a good and experienced, he will talk to the puppy and gain its confidence, while you hold the puppy and tell it how good and clever it is. With any luck, it will not even notice the needle going in, and it should be rewarded with an extra cuddle and a titbit when it is all over. Some vets are so good that dogs even welcome a visit to them, and they should be highly valued. If you are dissatisfied, we suggest that you change your vet.

From a few weeks of age your puppy should be accustomed to being examined. Say "mouth" or "teeth", and gently pull back the lips so that its teeth can be examined. Do not attempt to make this a full dental examination at first. Just a touch of its lips and words of praise when it submits is sufficient. Gradually increase the

A Rottweiler should be neither frightened of other creatures, nor aggressive towards them.
extent of the examination until it is accepted as a normal part of life; this will be
made easier if it is always praised and rewarded for good behaviour. The same
methods should be used for eyes, ears, testicles and general body examination.

We have already emphasised the need to accustom your puppy to all the domestic
sights and sounds. The same applies to experiences which you may not be able to
provide within your house and garden. Horses, sheep and cattle, chickens and small
animals should be met, and the dog must be taught that it must neither be frightened
by, nor aggressive towards such creatures. Even more important is the need for such
training with children and other humans, and this can cause problems. A dog is able
to sense fear and apprehension in humans, even if they show no outward signs.
Sensational media reports, particularly in Britain, have meant that many people,
especially children, have become frightened of Rottweilers even when the dog is
perfectly behaved. The mere fact that it is a Rottweiler is sufficient. At the same
time, you may also be worried that your dog may snap, and your apprehension will
literally go down the lead. You now have the situation where your young dog,
already worried by unusual circumstances, senses that you are nervous and that the
strange child is also nervous. Understandably, the dog responds by being nervous as
well, and the result is that the dog shows aggression and snaps. The fears and
apprehensions of all three parties are confirmed and become permanent. The

problem is to instil confidence in everyone involved. While there may be regrettable exceptions, confident people are rarely bitten by confident dogs. It normally takes fear on at least one side for someone to be bitten.

There is little you can do about the general public's attitude towards the Rottweiler, except ensure that your Rottweiler is an excellent ambassador for the breed, playing a part in dispelling the unfair image that it has acquired. Your job is to acquire confidence, so that while you are always aware of the potential of your dog, you give the impression that you are confident. The most common indication of your apprehension is that you tighten the lead. This is understandable: you do not want the dog to lunge, so you pull the lead up short. However, the dog feels the lead tighten and immediately starts looking for the problem. While you may keep the lead short to give you control, you must also ensure that it is not tight.

The dog's initial introduction to strangers, whatever their age, should be to people who are calm and confident. Avoid the nervous child who flaps its hands at the dog, snatching them back when the dog approaches closer. The dog's natural reaction is to grab at this object being waved under its nose. Whether your dog is meeting other animals or strange humans, your aim should be to achieve familiarity under calm, confident conditions, with an immediate sharp reprimand at any sign of aggression, followed, if possible, by a friendly introduction and reassurance that there is no need for any apprehension.

One of the less desirable traits of some Rottweilers, probably stemming from their herding and hunting forefathers, is a desire to chase anything moving and to grab at anything that moves past. Both these instincts should be discouraged, and, in our opinion, stock that shows a strong inclination to chase and to make sudden excitable grabs should not be bred from. For this reason we do not approve of some "tests for working ability", which include an object being dragged through the bushes in front of the dog, with the requirement that the dog should immediately show a desire to pursue it. While everyone knows that the object is only a bunch of rags on a string, in real life it could be a child or a domestic animal.

Closely akin to chasing and grabbing is the Rottweiler's habit of mouthing – taking your hand or arm in its mouth and holding it without actually biting. We do not really object to this, although we must admit that the difference between mouthing and biting may be a little obscure to the non-Rottweiler person. In the same way that a human baby explores the use of its hands by gripping and holding, a puppy uses its mouth. When our puppies try their teeth on our ankles, we respond with a loud yell of annoyance, and the puppy quickly learns not to do it again. The habit of mouthing persists with adult Rottweilers; it is probably nothing more than a desire to hold you, and in some way to show affection. However, the habit can easily

A well-trained Rott will live in harmony with other dogs – no matter how big or small.....

be misconstrued, so we suggest that you discourage it. You must take every possible opportunity to familiarize your young Rottweiler with the world that it has to live in. In Britain, we have found that the Exemption Show, which is usually coupled with a country fair involving other animals and crowds of relaxed people, is an excellent place to take your puppy. Shows like this can usually be found within a few miles of your home almost every summer weekend. Many include horses, sheep, poultry and other livestock; and there are always crowds of people, many of them with their dogs, enjoying the fun of the fair. Most of these shows place no restrictions on the age of the dogs; you do not have to book in advance; and unless you feel that you and your youngster are ready for the experience, you do not have to enter in the dog show section. You will find that many of the crowd will want to talk to your puppy, and because they will be people who like and understand animals, your dog will enjoy meeting them. Make it a happy day for your dog – not too much nagging and training, but lots of encouragement and fun. The main components of training and developing the character of your Rottweiler are: love and affection, encouragement, bribery or what you may prefer to describe as rewards for good behaviour; firm, prompt retribution for sins committed, followed by an immediate return to a happy atmosphere, and above all - endless patience. At five to six months of age your Rottweiler should be confident and willing to face new experiences with you. It should be trustful of you, your family, and of other people who do not give any obvious cause for alarm. The dog should believe that the world is a place where it can live happily, without the need to show undue aggression or apprehension. It should accept that its relationship to you is subordinate, although based on love and affection from both sides.

Chapter Four

GENERAL TRAINING

By now we hope that you have a young dog who embodies all the good aspects of the Rottweiler, and none of the potentially bad temperamental faults. If you have laid the foundations properly you should now be able to progress to more advanced and formal training, and your adult Rottweiler can develop into a dog to be proud of. In this chapter we are looking at this type of training from the dog's viewpoint, as well as examining your own approach and attitude.

First, let us look at some of the things that neither you nor your Rottweiler should do. You should be using every opportunity to take your dog out in public places, but it should not be allowed off the lead at such times. You may have achieved perfect control and heel work, and you may feel confident to walk through the crowded shopping centre with your dog trotting close to your side – a wonderful exhibition of well-trained Rottweiler. Regrettably, not all of us are as good as we would like to think we are. Something happens to make your Rott forget his training – and you and your Rottweiler are in trouble. In Britain, as Rottweilers have found to their cost, when a dog offends as a result of human irresponsibility, the dog is killed while the human gets off much more lightly. Obviously we are not advocating capital punishment for irresponsible dog ownership, but you should never lose sight of the fact that the ultimate responsibility for your dog's behaviour lies with yourself. Your Rottweiler may be behaving perfectly – and suddenly become the victim of an unprovoked attack. The nature of the breed means that the dog is bound to respond, and invariably, it will then be blamed for the whole incident. It is highly regrettable, but Rottweiler owners must face the fact that in any incident that involves a Rottweiler, there will be bias against the Rott. You must therefore avoid giving the opposition any ammunition, however unfair it may be to you and your dog. Your ego as an able trainer is of far less importance than the good name of the breed. So, Rottweilers should be kept on the lead in public places, even in city parks where other dog owners, less responsible than you, may let their dogs run free.

There are a number of problems associated with keeping and exercising a big dog with the character of the Rottweiler in a crowded urban environment, and we are tempted to say that you should not keep a Rottweiler unless you live in the country with a reasonably large well-fenced garden. However, this would be unfair to the many devoted Rottweiler lovers who keep their dogs in small houses in the city. We know of people with perfectly trained and delightful Rottweilers living in upstairs flats, but they are conscientious, experienced owners who work very hard to ensure that their dogs live happy, normal lives. You should certainly not keep a Rottweiler if your garden, however big, is not adequately fenced. All dogs tend to be territorial and a Rottweiler will very quickly decide to dominate the neighbourhood if he is allowed to roam at will. Once again, we would emphasise that you have a duty to your dog, to the breed and to the community to ensure that your dog is kept under proper control. This applies not only to the training that you give your Rottweiler, but also to the way that your home and premises are organised. For example, unless you are prepared to live without visits from the milkman, the postman and other callers, you must make sure that visitors can approach your front door without meeting your Rottweiler on the porch.

Fouling of pavements and other public places has become socially unacceptable. Even less popular is the fouling of your non-doggy neighbour's front lawns. All too often we hear complaints about the dog owner who regularly takes the dog for a walk and allows it to make use of everyone's front lawn except his own. Dogs do not live in the community by divine right, and unless dog lovers recognise this, we shall find more and more restrictions placed on our dogs and on their owners. It is useless to argue that dog excrement is biodegradable and that our dogs are responsible for far less pollution than humans. Dog fouling has been seized on by the anti-dog lobby as a very effective weapon, and their exaggerated and often untrue allegations have received the support of local government and health bodies. So, make arrangements to be able to pick up after your dog.

Many people like to keep two or more Rottweilers. If you intend that your dogs are to live in the house under normal domestic arrangements, then we would strongly advise that you do not attempt to keep two males. We would be the first to admit that very occasionally someone breaks this rule and gets away with it. This is usually when the owners are outstanding trainers who have achieved a totally dominant position over their dogs. For the rest of us, a pair of male Rottweilers almost certainly means that at some stage there will be a dispute over who is top dog. A fight between two fully grown Rottweiler males is something to be avoided at all costs. Of course, if you are breeding and showing Rottweilers with a number of stud dogs and a properly organised kennel set up, you will be able to keep your males apart.

Some people, especially men, like to indulge in wrestling games with their dog. It can be fun with a young dog, and you may argue that it is harmless. To the dog it soon becomes a test of superiority and he will eventually become aggressive and determined to win. At this stage you will give up on the grounds that the dog is getting excited and out of hand. You may consider that you have parted as equals with the honours even. To the dog he will have won, and he will consider that he has taken another step towards establishing his dominance over you. For the same reason we do not like the 'tug-toys' with a handle at each end, one for the dog to grip and one for the owner. The human is the stronger, but inevitably he will let go first, and as far as the dog is concerned, this is another victory.

If the need to earn a living means that your Rottweiler is left shut up in the house from early morning until the evening, by which time you are probably too tired to take him for a walk, then we would suggest that you deny yourself the pleasure of owning this breed. A young puppy certainly needs attention throughout the day, for feeding, house training and companionship. Leaving a puppy shut up for some eight hours, returning to a soiled and chewed-up room, and then punishing it for something done many hours ago – which was largely your fault – is not the way to rear a Rottweiler, or any other dog. Of course, your dog should get used to being left alone without misbehaving, but it should get used to this gradually. It may pay you to build an outside kennel and run for your adult dog to use during the day, so that it can watch the world go by. However, you will not be popular with the neighbours if the dog spends its day barking at them. The Rottweiler is a dog which needs and responds to human companionship. The more time you spend together, the better the relationship between you.

We consider that the tug-toy is one of the more stupid products of the pet industry,

Rottweilers love to play, but be careful in your choice of toys. This fly-ball game is fun for both dog and owner.

but this does not mean that your Rottweiler should not have toys. On the contrary, toys are as much a part of your dog's upbringing as they are to children. Whether you buy from the enormous range of dog toys available at your local pet shop, or whether you improvise with old socks and worn-out tennis balls, is up to you. We have long believed that most commercial toys are designed to appeal to you rather than to your dog. Toys have three main functions: they serve as a training aid to teach a dog to retrieve and to search, a distraction to persuade the dog to chew the toy rather than your best shoes or the leg of the table, and they can be used purely as a plaything. The best training-aid toy for a puppy is an old sock stuffed with rags. From a very early age your youngster can be taught to retrieve it and bring it to hand, or to search and recover it from under the furniture when it has been mislaid. This training must be accompanied with lots of verbal encouragement and praise each time the dog is successful. Toys that can be chewed, as an alternative to chewing your possessions, are essential. Apart from chewing to relieve the discomfort of teething, a young dog will also chew to alleviate boredom and as a result of nervous stress such as being left alone in the house. It is rather like a human twiddling his thumbs. Remember that what you can do with your fingers, a dog can only do with his mouth. The answer is to provide plenty of different toys and to

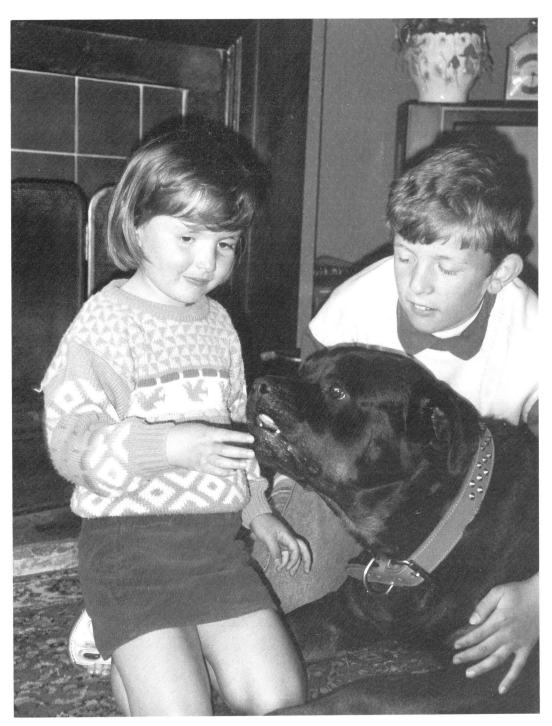

The Rottweiler responds to human companionship.

make it clear that, while the dog is welcome to chew its own toys, it must leave your possessions alone. Chew toys for Rottweilers need to be substantial; those powerful jaws can quickly reduce most things to bite-size pieces. You must also make sure that if it does swallow the bits they are of a substance that can be digested. Large marrow bones are probably the best answer. Play toys can be whatever turns your dog on. One of our males chooses a large galvanized bucket. He will carry it around, bash it against the wall and use it as a football. Others enjoy bits of wood, old rubber tyres, soft plastic bottles, which make a lovely rattle when jumped on, and empty cardboard boxes. Squeaky rubber toys are popular, but the squeak does not tend to last very long. It is a good idea to keep indoor toys in a toy box. We use a wastepaper bin, and when we ask a dog to find, it carefully examines what is on offer in the basket and then pulls out the one it wants.

You may be tempted to avoid all the problems of rearing and training a young Rottweiler, by acquiring an adult in the hope that someone else will have done all the work for you. Unless you are both very careful and lucky, this will not be successful. There are always a small number of adult Rottweilers well brought up and well bred who, through no fault of their own, are looking for new homes. If you are lucky enough to find one of these then by all means take it in and give it the good home that it deserves. You will have done a kindness to the dog and to the breed. However, the majority of adult dogs on offer are only available because something has gone wrong. Their owners may have failed to bring them up correctly, they may have deliberately encouraged the Rottweiler's aggressive and guarding instincts, or the dog may have been bred from the wrong type of parents. Most of these dogs are beyond redemption. It is a sad fact that many excellent Rottweilers, who have been perfect examples of the breed, have died because a small number of bad dogs have been allowed to live. These 'bad apples' have harmed the breed's reputation to such an extent that some people have lost confidence in their Rottweilers, even though their dog may have an exemplary temperament and has never transgressed. As a result innocent dogs have been put down. It is far kinder to the breed to destroy dogs that have attacked and bitten humans without good cause, than to allow them to live and probably do the same thing again. Once a Rottweiler has been allowed to develop bad habits there are very few owners who are capable of effecting a change. If they do succeed, it is almost certain that the dog will have to live a very restricted life. Breeders and owners who re-house such dogs, instead of having them put down, are only evading their responsibilities and passing on to others an unpleasant task which they should carry out themselves. So, as a general rule, we would advise you to avoid giving a home to an older dog unless you are quite certain why it is available and that it is the type of dog you want to own. It is much better to start with a puppy and bring it up the way that you want it to be. One final thing that you should not do. We have already mentioned the Rottweiler's natural guarding instincts: without any special encouragement it will protect you and your family – and there is nothing wrong in wishing to own a dog with this capability. However, unless you have a special need for an extremely tough guard dog and are capable of controlling such a dog and are prepared to keep him under very restricted circumstances, you should not encourage the guarding and aggressive instincts of your Rottweiler in any way. Many people encourage their young dog to "get him" or "get it", in the belief that it is necessary to train their dog to protect them. As we have said, your dog's instinct to guard will be quite sufficient for normal domestic purposes. We would go further and suggest that to either own or train a dog of any breed, and especially one with the characteristics of a Rottweiler, in 'man work', or what ever other euphemism you care to use, should require a special licence in the same way as a gun. Many people will cite the German Schutzhund working tests as an example of useful and beneficial testing and training. In Europe, we have seen many magnificent examples of Schutzhund-trained Rottweilers who are a credit both to the breed and their trainers. In Britain there have also been a number of Rottweilers who have qualified as 'Patrol Dog' (PD), which includes a man work qualification; again these dogs have given no cause for concern. However, it is easy to lose sight of the enormous amount of obedience and control training and testing required before there is any question of attack training. British enthusiasts for Schutzhund training have shown a desire to carry out the attack aspects of the training without laying the necessary foundation of control and obedience. They then wonder why the dog starts to show undue aggression. To argue, as some of them do, that Schutzhund training is a sport and that the dog considers it to be a game, can only be described as ignorant rubbish. Unless Britain is prepared to establish the rigid control of both instructors and testing used by the Germans and other European countries, man work is best left to the experts such as the police and armed forces.

By now, you are probably wondering whether owning a Rottweiler is worth all the effort. If you have any doubts then we suggest that you do not. In the hands of those who love and understand these dogs, there is no better breed. However, ownership of a Rottweiler involves hard work, understanding, and above all, taking on a considerable responsibility. If all this is too much for you or does not fit into your lifestyle then you should not own a Rottweiler.

There are a number of training aids available, some of them are excellent while others can only be given qualified approval. The basic means of control for a Rottweiler has, for many years, been a good strong leather lead and a fairly heavy check chain. This combination has two advantages: firstly the whole outfit is strong enough to hold a Rott, provided, of course, that you have enough strength to hold on to your end; and secondly the choking effect of the chain helps to give you control and compensates for any lack of muscle on your part. We should emphasise, though, that the aim of a check chain is not to strangle your dog into submission. The art of using any type of slip lead or check chain is to administer a quick jerk accompanied by the command "heel" whenever the dog pulls, followed by an immediate slackening of the lead. Prolonged tightening of the chain will merely result in a half-choked dog fighting to escape. The aim of check-chain training is to instil in the dog the knowledge that a slight tightening of the chain portends a sharper and more painful jerk. As a result, the dog learns to avoid the jerk by ceasing to pull.

The check chain is still widely used, but it has some disadvantages. If it is not used with care the effect can be excessively harsh. A thin chain or one that is jerked too hard can cause pain and injury, and the chain itself can wear away the hair around the neck causing an unsightly mark. The dog cannot be allowed to run free and unsupervised while wearing the chain because of the risk that the chain can become caught up in something and strangle him. The maximum control is achieved when the chain is high on the dog's neck, just behind the ears. However, in order to put the chain over the dog's head the chain has to be longer than the circumference of the neck at this point. This means that when the lead and chain are slack, the chain drops back towards the dog's shoulder, and the next time you require to tighten the chain to achieve control, it is in the wrong place and does not work effectively. An effective alternative to the check chain is what is known in Britain as the 'American collar' or 'control collar'. This consists of a collar, usually of strong round nylon cord. At one end there is a ring and at the other end a normal spring-loaded lead-clip. A second ring runs freely up and down the length of the cord. The collar is cut to measure so that it fits closely around the neck, just behind the ears, but without undue restriction when the spring clip is fastened to the free-running ring. The lead is then attached to the other ring. The effect is that the collar remains up behind the ears where it is most efficient when pulled, while still giving the handler the ability to use the tightening effect as a means of control.

As far as leads are concerned, we still prefer a flat leather lead, using whatever length suits you. We find that the ideal length is between three and four feet; this is long enough for you to allow the dog to stand away from you, and you can wind it around your hand if you need to shorten it. We do not like the flat nylon leads which tend to cut into your hands. A further aid to control is the long nylon cord lead wound around a spring-loaded drum contained in a plastic handle. The spring-loaded drum means that the lead automatically shortens when the tension is taken off, while any lengthening of the lead can be controlled by a button-operated brake contained in the handle. This device is useful for allowing your dog to have a reasonable amount of exercise, while you retain control. The automatic shortening of the lead, as tension is removed, solves the problem of the dog becoming tangled in a long lead, while allowing him freedom of movement. This is also a useful aid to teaching the recall. We have found that the rather bulky plastic handle is somewhat clumsy and uncomfortable, but this is probably unavoidable. If you have to exercise your dog in a public place such as a park, we would recommend this type of lead.

Another type of control aid is what is usually described as a 'head collar'. This is an arrangement of light nylon straps resembling a loose-fitting muzzle, although it does not really act as one, with the lead attachment ring towards the end of the dog's nose. A pull on the lead turns the dog's head in the direction of the pull; it literally has to follow its nose. This device certainly helps to control your dog, but it does little to further its training. Furthermore, it is rather flimsy and a dog can use his paws to remove it. We would not be happy using a head collar as the sole means of control for a powerful dog, and we would prefer to have a check chain also attached to the lead as a reserve. None of these aids should be considered as providing the complete answer to the control of your Rottweiler; they should be viewed as a means of assistance. The aim is to have a dog that is completely under your control by means of your verbal commands, continuing to obey the last command until it is replaced by another one. These commands should include one that indicates that he can relax and go and have fun for a while.

All commands should be given in a clear, sharp tone so that there is no doubt in the dog's mind that it is a command and not just a friendly chat. Later, when your dog is well trained, you may be able to give commands in a quiet voice, but not in the initial stages. Equally, you will achieve nothing by losing your temper and yelling at the dog. It will become nervous and unsettled and in no mood to absorb training. Neither should you constantly nag at the dog, either by your voice or by jerking at the lead. Your own concentration is important: you should try and anticipate what your dog is about to do, and give a corrective command if necessary. You must establish in your own mind what commands you are going to use for each action, and stick to them. Rottweilers can learn to speak English, but only with a fairly limited vocabulary, and you cannot expect them to obey several different words for the same action. An example of this is the command "Sit", which should mean sit and not lie down. If you vary this command by saying "Sit Down", you may understand that the words mean the same thing, but if your dog has learnt the two separate commands, it will either become confused, or it will decide that you don't know what you want! Praise is important. Every exercise that is successfully

A team of obedient Rottweilers.   *Pearce.*

completed, however small, should be greeted with lots of enthusiastic praise and encouragement. You should not be inhibited by what others may think if you go into an extravagant burst of congratulations when your dog has done what you wanted. Do not forget what we have said about bribery – a titbit given after a successful exercise will go a long way to consolidate your training.

A training programme should be as varied as possible and you should not allow the dog to become bored. It is very tempting to repeat a lesson over and over again when your dog has just learnt what to do, just to prove to yourself how clever you are. Your Rottweiler, with its intelligence, will probably make it clear that having completed the exercise twice, it sees no reason to do it a third time. If at any time your dog fails in an exercise, you should continue until it has at least shown some understanding of what is required. Then you can praise the dog, and save further progress for another session. The number of training exercises your Rottweiler must learn in order to live happily under normal domestic circumstances is quite small. The dog must come when it is called; stop what it is doing on the command 'No'; walk calmly at your side both on and off the lead; sit or lie down when ordered; stay in one place – either at the 'sit' or the 'down' – while you move away from him, including moving out of sight; and it must surrender to you any object which it has, on command. Obviously there are many more exercises involving more advanced

Rottweilers can be trained to live in harmony with all members of the family – even when this includes a pack of hounds!

work, but none of these should be undertaken until the basic training is well established. A puppy should be taught to respond to his name at the very beginning of its training. At first you should call the dog from a distance of only a couple of feet, using its name followed by the command "Come". This command should be given in a gentle and encouraging tone of voice, implying that coming to you will be a pleasure. A harsh voice will probably send him in the opposite direction. It may also help if you sit or crouch down, as this will make you appear much more friendly than if you are towering over a small puppy. Gradually increase the distance you call from, and remember to give lots of praise and encouragement, plus the reward of a titbit when the exercise is successfully completed.

Heel work, by which we mean the dog walking at your side either on or off the lead, is usually done with the dog on your left side. As far as we know, there is no particular reason for choosing the left-side; it is just that everyone, everywhere, adopts this practice. Certainly it has nothing to do with traffic movement, as it applies in countries which drive on the left and in those that drive on the right. Familiarity with a collar and lead should have started for your puppy at an early age. The command to use is "Heel". Position the dog on your left hand side with its shoulder against your leg. The clever bit is to maintain the dog's attention so that it enjoys moving with you in this position. Talk to the dog, pat your leg, rattle something in your pocket. If the dog pulls ahead, draw it back repeating the command "Heel", and praise it the moment it is back in position. Make sure that you walk in a straight line and that the dog walks alongside you rather than you walking alongside your dog. When you stop, the dog should stop close to you – do not try and cheat on this by stepping in to your dog.

In the initial stages of lead training it does not matter too much what position your dog adopts when you both stop; the important thing is to get it walking quietly at your side and responsive to your wishes by remaining close and not pulling out in front, to one side, or lagging behind. However, at some stage you have got to decide on the position that you want your dog to adopt when it is walking at your side and you stop moving. For normal domestic life we feel that it is best if the dog sits when you stop, unless you have plans for a show career, in which case you may prefer that it remains at the stand. In the show ring it is easy to spot the obedience-trained dog who shows how well trained it is by sitting at the very moment that the owner wants it to stand and show to its best advantage. There has always been a certain amount of controversy between those who claim, quite rightly, that a show dog can be trained to stand on command, and those who point out that in the show ring the 'stand' you want is a pose – the dog drawn up to his full height with an alert stare into the distance – rather than the slightly crouched, waiting to obey the next command, 'stand' of the obedience-trained dog. These are decisions that you must make for yourself, depending on the future you want for your dog. However, if you are planning a show career for your Rottweiler you must not make the mistake of assuming that only show training is necessary. The basic control exercises are still a vital part of your dog's upbringing. Teaching your dog to walk correctly on the lead will take considerable time and require daily practice. At the same time you must not turn every minute of your daily walks into one long drill session. Make certain that they are fun things for your dog to do, as well as a time to learn.

The "Sit" exercise has the advantage that it can be taught at quiet moments indoors in the comfort of your lounge or kitchen. Like all dog training the actual exercise is not complicated, but it requires frequent repetition before the lesson is absorbed. The aim is to get the rear end of the dog to go down while the front remains upright. While a dog will sit naturally, they tend to prefer to either lie down or stand up. Sitting is little more than an intermediate position between the two. The secret is to keep the head up, either by holding it up with your hand under the chin or by holding the head up by using the lead. At the same time exert downward pressure on the hindquarters by gently pressing down with the other hand. As you press downwards the hand under the chin should move upwards. All this should be accompanied by the command "Sit", given as a sharp command. Be patient and gentle with this exercise, as it is easy to make your dog panic when he finds that you are interfering with his geometry. While this is the traditional method of teaching the sit, there are reasons why we do not like it. For a start, a Rottweiler's weight and quick growth-rate means that puppies may have a number of bone and muscle problems, and we do not like to run the risk of adding to them by pushing and pulling at a growing youngster. In the show ring many judges will push down on the hindquarters to test the dog's strength and soundness. If a dog has been taught to sit by this method, you cannot blame the dog if it responds to the judge's pressure by sitting. In fact, many Rottweilers will push back when they feel pressure on their hindquarters, and this is a characteristic which we would prefer not to change. There is an alternative method of teaching the sit, which we recommend. Hold the dog's head up and use your other hand to push forward on its hind legs, just above the hocks. This makes the dog lower its hindquarters into a sitting position – rather like folding up a collapsible garden chair. Do not forget to praise the dog for a successful exercise. The down position follows logically from the sit. Start from the sitting position and place one hand on the dog's shoulder. Give the command "Down", and press gently downwards, at the same time using your other hand to point towards the floor. You may find that you have to reinforce this movement by gently pulling the dog's front legs towards you. It is immaterial whether it goes down on all-fours or lies on its side. Remember that your dog will feel vulnerable in the down position. It is being forced into a submissive posture and it will be reassured if you bend down so you are on the same level. It will also need lots of praise and reassurance. Keep "sits" and "downs" short in the early stages and have plenty of play periods in between.

The methods we have outlined were largely developed by professional trainers who needed to establish quick and effective training routines. To a considerable extent such methods rely on constantly telling the dog what it must not do, and on the assumption that a dog's motivation is the same as a human's. In other words, the handler fails to think like a dog. We have a lot of sympathy with one of the more able of the dog behaviour experts who points out that if your dog persists in soiling your bed every day then the answer is quite simple: close the bedroom door. The dog, unable to make its daily expression of opinion, goes outside where it belongs and is rewarded for it. The basis of this approach to training is that misdemeanours are virtually ignored on the principle that constant nagging does little to solve the problem, and can be counter-productive; correct behaviour is rewarded with enormous praise and the material award of titbits. The method can be summarised as: "Wait until you dog does what you want, and then reward and praise it."

When you apply these ideas to the "Sit" and "Down" exercises, it is a case of encouraging, rather than forcing, the dog into the required position and then rewarding it. The dog quickly learns that adopting the required position on command produces goodies rather like feeding coins into a slot machine. In fact, the dog is probably convinced that it has trained you to produce a titbit every time it sits! If your dog is standing close in front of you, expecting the biscuit that you have in your hand, and if you then take a pace closer, the dog will almost certainly go into a half-crouch. It is forced to do this because your forward movement has made it move its forelegs backwards, while its back legs have remained in the same position. This half-crouch is halfway to a sit. If you couple this with the command "Sit" and the reward, you will very quickly have your dog sitting on command, without a lot of pushing and pulling to get it into position. A similar method can be used for the down. When the dog is sitting, crouch in front of it and move the biscuit down to ground level; the dog will soon learn to lower its front end down to biscuit level. Methods such as these may not work with every Rottweiler, but they are certainly worth trying and are preferable to the confrontational "do it or else" approach.

An essential second stage to both the "sit" and the "down" positions is the "stay". This quite simply means that the dog remains in the required posture, on the same spot, until the release command is given. At first, the dog will be inclined to break away the moment you remove your restraining hand, even after it has gone into the desired position, so keep your hand in position and use the command " Stay". Gradually you can relax the restraint while repeating the command. Slowly, only a foot at a time, you can move backwards. Repeat the command "Stay" only when the dog shows signs of moving. Again, this exercise requires lots of patience and practice. When you are repeating the command "Stay", do not use the dog's name. Remember that you have trained the dog to come to you when you call its name. Secondly, avoid eye contact while it is at the stay. The dog will probably be looking at you, awaiting your next command. Eye contact will make the dog come to you. Initially, always return to the dog's side before releasing it from the stay. Eventually you will be able to call the dog to you from a distance, from the stay position, but it needs to be very steady before you do this. When you do release the dog, let it enjoy a good play period before you continue training.

We have only attempted to cover those basic training exercises which you and your Rottweiler need in order to live a happy life together. There are many more activities which you can both enjoy, and we hope that you will progress to more advanced work such as obedience competition, working trials and agility. In any case, we would suggest that you join a club which provides training facilities, preferably a Rottweiler breed club, so that you are training with people who are having the same problems as yourself and with trainers who understand the Rottweiler. This gives you the chance to meet and be advised by knowledgeable people, and a well organised club will also be able to provide equipment such as jumps and agility obstacles. Another advantage of attending a weekly class is that at least once a week you and your dog have to get down to some work. At home it is all too easy to put it off until tomorrow. However, attending a training class does not mean that you can neglect your homework. Daily practice is essential.

If you do attend a training class you should resist any attempt by the instructor, especially if he is one who is not experienced with Rottweilers, to take your dog from you and demonstrate how an exercise should be done. For a start, this is a confidence trick. Any dog who finds a stranger on the end of his lead will, for a few minutes, be mentally off-balance and will obey until it has weighed up the new situation. It looks as if the instructor has a magic formula, but in fact the dog will revert to its old habits as soon as it gets its confidence back or is returned to you. Insist that you keep the lead and that the instructor tells you what to do, and in this way both you and the dog will learn the lesson. Obviously not every instructor is perfect, and some will try and use methods which you may object to. Do not allow either yourself or your dog to be bullied. There are plenty of good trainers and training classes available. If you do not like the methods used, say so, and find another trainer.

Unless there is no possible alternative, you should not send your Rottweiler away for training. You will find it is both expensive and of little value. Your dog will be trained to obey someone else's commands, and there is no guarantee that it will obey you. You may even find that the dog that comes back to you is no longer the dog you want. While there are some excellent trainers available, there are also a lot of bad ones who charge high prices for a poor job. The best trainers will tell you that the ideal is for you and your dog to train together, and to enjoy working together and the satisfaction that comes from success.

A well trained Rottweiler can be a source of great pleasure to you, and to those that you live with. It can be a valuable ambassador for the breed and for dogs in general. A Rottweiler that is wrongly trained, or not trained at all, can only be described as an unexploded bomb – and all too often the bomb goes off.

Chapter Five

PRACTICAL CARE

We have discussed the character of the Rottweiler and how a Rottweiler owner should train and develop that character. We now move on to the dog's physical welfare with regard to housing, feeding and general care.

The best prevention against disease is a healthy dog. Good health starts with a suitable diet, regular exercise, cleanliness and a warm dry bed. It is also obvious that you should make full use of modern science with its wide range of preventative medicines and vaccines, but these are not in themselves a substitute for tender loving care. The Rottweiler is a sound, sensible dog without any exaggerated breed points introduced by man, which can give rise to problems in some breeds. Regretfully, it is subject to a few hereditary conditions, which cannot really be attributed to the requirements of the Breed Standard, and these will be dealt with in a later chapter. However, the Rottweiler's physical characteristics can cause problems, especially during the early stages of growth. Relative to its adult weight, a Rottweiler puppy is normally born very small. Many breeds which are smaller than the Rottweiler when fully grown, produce new-born puppies which are, on average, larger than

Rottweiler puppies. The result of this is that Rott puppies have a very rapid growth rate. A puppy's weight will double each week for the first three weeks and continue to increase at the rate of half its weight per week for several weeks after that. It will probably weigh in the region of 14 to 15lbs by the age of eight weeks. An increase in weight of this magnitude on a body where bone and muscle are not fully developed can lead to orthopaedic problems, some of which are not apparent until later in life. For this reason we do not like the fat butter-ball puppy much admired by puppy visitors and prefer ours to be fairly lean, although not, of course, skinny and undernourished.

PUPPY DIET

In the past we were not enthusiastic about the various 'all-in-one' diets on the market, but we must admit that some of the modern ones, especially those designed for puppy rearing, seem to be excellent. We do not like the use of 'constant access' hoppers, as we consider them to be an undesirable and lazy method of puppy rearing, which avoids the frequent attention and supervision which is necessary. We like our puppies fed in quantities which they clear up in a few seconds; we hate to see half-eaten dishes of food lying around puppy pens. If you are not willing to prepare carefully balanced meals several times a day for four or five months, then you should not be rearing a Rottweiler litter.

Our puppy diet used to be based on good-quality minced meat – beef, chicken or lamb – mixed with wholemeal biscuit, plus milk-feeds made from one of the milk substitutes that are specially manufactured for puppies. These meals can be varied by the occasional use of cooked fish or scrambled eggs. Some people give drinks of cow's milk, but we have found it has a laxative effect, and we prefer to use it cooked in some form of milk pudding, such as custard or rice. This method of rearing requires the very careful use of supplements such as cod liver oil and bone meal, and does require considerable experience. The excessive use of vitamin and mineral supplements can cause permanent damage and, contrary to past beliefs, the surplus is not always excreted.

The modern all-in-one foods take most of the guess-work out of puppy rearing; supplements are included at the correct level and they are clean and labour-saving. We should, however, point out that although manufacturers list the proportions of protein, carbohydrate etc. contained in their product, they do not give the sources. For example: protein can be animal, vegetable, or even manufactured artificially. We are inclined to wonder whether artificial protein contains all the desirable elements which you would find in a lump of beef. Expiry dates of such products are also important. Some of the additives have a short shelf-life, and there may be a question about the effect of some of the preservatives used. When you are choosing a diet for your dog, you face the same problems as when you are selecting your own food. Cost, availability and ease of handling have to be weighed against nutritional value, the effect of artificial additives and colouring, and the benefits of a natural diet. As with your own diet, the final decision must be yours.

EXERCISE

Because of the Rottweiler's weight/muscle development ratio, you should not allow your puppy to slide around on highly polished or slippery floors, or let it jump down from heights. Clambering up the stairs will do no harm to a sturdy adventurous youngster, but hurtling down again, jumping the last three steps and then sliding across the polished floor can easily cause injury. We believe in free exercise for our puppies, and a certain number of bumps and bruises are inevitable – it all helps to produce an adult sound in body and mind. However, such exercise must be applied with care and commonsense.

The feet of a puppy that is reared indoors can be adversely affected by floor surfaces. If its feet only come into contact with a soft carpet indoors and a grass lawn outside, then its feet will spread and its nails will become excessively long. The nails can be clipped, but the real answer to good feet comes firstly from breeding, and secondly from the nails being worn down by exercise on a variety of rough surfaces. A dog who has the correct 'cat-like' feet will keep its nails short by natural wear, provided that it spends some time on rough uneven surfaces. Part of its outdoor play time should therefore be spent in areas surfaced with concrete, paving stones or gravel.

BEDDING

Dogs spend a lot of time sleeping, and their bed is therefore a matter of importance. If your dog lives in the house, it may make its own decision as to where it sleeps. This may be your bed or the best armchair, and you must decide whether to allow this or not. Even if you allow special privileges at certain times, we would suggest that you provide the dog with a bed of its own that can be occupied at all times, as a matter of right. A dog will also use its bed to store its treasures such as old bones – and this is not popular with guests if it chooses to keep them down the backs of your chairs! We have found that the best beds are the fibre-glass oval-shaped type. They are light, reasonably cheap to buy, easy to keep clean, and almost indestructible.

They do need several layers of blanket to soften their hardness, or better still, one of the washable dog duvets which are now available. If you buy this kind of bed, make sure that it is big enough for your dog when it is fully grown. If you buy one to fit your puppy you will very soon find that your growing dog is hanging out at both ends. You may be tempted by one of the big squishy bean bag type beds. They are very comfortable and the dogs love them – contrary to some opinions, dogs do appreciate a soft bed. However, they are difficult to keep clean and if your Rott decides to find out what is inside its bed, you will spend the rest of your life picking up the tiny pieces of filling. Feather-filled beds have the same fault, only worse. Your Rott's bed should be placed in a warm draught-proof corner where it is out of the way of passing feet. Remember that while your dog may want to lie close to the boiler in winter, it will probably prefer a cooler spot during the summer.

KENNELING

Any Rottweiler living outdoors requires a warm, strong and well designed kennel. This is a hardy breed, and given the proper accommodation, dogs will thrive even in very cold weather. This does not mean that a dog who has lived in a centrally heated house for the whole of its life can suddenly be moved into an unheated outdoor kennel in the middle of winter, but those who have lived outside from the beginning will be quite content and will even show signs of distress if required to live indoors.

Our outdoor kennels are built of insulated concrete blocks. Wooden kennels require far more maintenance, and they can be ruined in a few hours by a dog who decides to chew. Heat is also lost through the roof, so this requires insulation. The layout should consist of a sleeping area with an attached outside run, some of which may also be covered. The sleeping area should be large enough to contain a sleeping box with additional space for the dog to get out of the box to stretch its legs, and to relieve itself. We do not train our dogs that are in outside kennels to be kennel-clean. They may spend as much as twelve hours shut in this area during the winter, so they need plenty of space. The sleeping area should also be of sufficient height for you to work inside it without having to bend double. Ideally, you should also have electric light and the facility to plug in an electric heater. An emergency may arise, such as having to care for a sick dog, and you may have to spend a night in the kennel. The sleeping area should also have provision for a drinking bowl. Our Rottweilers delight in picking up water buckets and emptying the contents all over the floor! The ordinary commercial bucket rings merely meant that the dog demolished the ring as well as the bucket. We solved the problem by building an open-topped brick box into the corner of each kennel, just big enough to take a water bucket and about one inch higher than the bucket. We like to use covered sleeping boxes with a partly closed front in our outside kennels. These are made of fairly stout wood which helps the dog to conserve the heat that it generates. The sleeping area and the sleeping boxes are big enough to accommodate a pair of Rotts, both for company and mutual warmth. We use shredded paper for bedding, which can be bought by the bale and is easily stored. It does not break down into dust, which can get into a dog's eyes and coat in the way that hay or straw does, neither does it harbour insects. It does need to be shaken up each day and replaced fairly frequently, especially if it has become damp. After use it is easily disposed of by burning.

Each kennel should have its own concrete-floored individual run attached to it. Ours are about 12ft by 8ft. and open into the large grass exercising area. Our runs have concrete-block walls to a height of about four feet, topped with another two or three feet of heavy gauge weldmesh. Chain link fencing may be adequate for large runs, but it is useless for the small ones. A determined Rottweiler can soon reduce it to a tangle of wire. The solid concrete-block walls stop dogs trying to fight through the wire, but it also encourages them to stand on their hindlegs and even jump – a useful form of exercise for dogs kept in kennels. All gates and doors should be made of metal with strong bolts. We prefer both gate and door to open inwards. Letting a Rottweiler out in the morning when it is dying to see you and go for a run around the paddock means that you can be knocked flat on your back by an outward-opening door, if your dog hits the inside at the moment that you, on the outside, undo the bolts.

In our opinion, the kennel for your Rottweiler should be substantial, with no risk of the dog being able to break out. However, in New Zealand we saw an interesting alternative. Out there, the majority of Rottweilers are extremely well trained and they are expected to guard the property. These particular kennels had a very attractive range of buildings, each with its own attached run. The runs were made of lightweight ornamental wooden trellis. Any Rottweiler could have walked straight through it. The owner's explanation was: "Under normal circumstances the dog will accept that it stays in the run and makes no attempt to break out. However, should there be an intruder in the garden when we are not there, then they can, and will, break through the trellis. On the rare occasions that this has happened, the sight of the dogs breaking out has been sufficient for the the intruder to put himself on the other side of the perimeter fence, which is Rottweiler-proof." The idea seems to have some advantages, but we would prefer to have our Rotts in solid, secure kennels.

There are two things to take into account when deciding where to site a range of outdoor kennels: proximity to the house and shade from the sun. We have emphasised that the Rottweiler enjoys the company of its master, and you should make it as easy as possible to provide this companionship. We like our outdoor kennels to be close to our back door so that the dogs can see all our comings and goings. This also makes it possible to catch any sign of trouble at an early stage. Shade from the sun is important: your dog is far more likely to suffer discomfort and even death from the effects of the sun, than to suffer from the cold. A kennel and run from which the dog cannot escape, exposed to hours of summer sun, can be torture for any dog, especially a Rottweiler whose coat is primarily designed for fairly cold climates. Try and place your kennel block under the shade of a tree; and your large exercising paddock should also be sited to provide your dog with a choice of shade or sunshine.

ADULT DIET

The diet of your adult Rottweiler has to be a compromise between what may be the ideal diet and what is possible under modern conditions. For most of us the days have gone when it was possible to feed wholemeal biscuit and either fresh tripe or fresh meat to our dogs. Availability, cost and hygiene regulations have made such methods almost impossible. There are really three choices of feeding method available. Firstly what we would call the traditional method whereby you use a basic biscuit, preferably wholemeal, together with a source of meat protein such as meat or tripe probably cooked and frozen. Secondly, you can use a tinned dog food, which may be meat, fish, or vegetarian, plus some sort of biscuit. Thirdly, there are the 'all-in-one' diets. There is a wide range of prepared and frozen meats on the market for dogs. Some of them are precisely what they claim to be, others are more suspect. The modern human food processing industry does not leave very much over to be used for dog food and some of what is offered is literally the sweepings off the abattoir floor, which after it has been minced, cooked, coloured and advertised appears to be, and probably is, an appetising and acceptable diet for a dog. We always admire the courage of dog food salesmen who claim that their product is fit for human consumption and prove it by eating it! In America, labelling on petfood is more detailed than in Britain and products must carry a Guaranteed Analysis which states the maximum or minimum amount of nutrients contained in the food. We have always taken an interest in what our dog food really contains, and apart from asking the manufacturers, which seldom produces any useful answers, we have found that as far as frozen blocks of food are concerned, it pays to put the first block of food into boiling water so that it breaks down into its constituent parts.

We were once offered some very appetising blocks of what was claimed to be frozen turkey meat. Soaking revealed that what we had was largely ground up feathers and bone. The birds had been skinned, the flesh removed and the bone, skin and feathers ground up and frozen into blocks. While it is true to say that feathers contain a considerable amount of protein, we were not prepared to use them to feed our dogs. We discovered that another product, described as a baked biscuit, contained large quantities of dried fruit and cherries, plus numerous small pieces of coloured plastic. A visit to the factory revealed enormous heaps of stale bread, cakes and buns, many of them still in their original plastic wrappings. The whole lot, wrappings and all, were broken up in a machine and then baked and packed into sacks printed with instructions and claims as to its feeding value. We must admit that, used as a basic biscuit with the addition of tripe or meat, it seemed an adequate maintenance diet, but it could hardly be described as a carefully balanced one.

As with the puppy diets, the high quality, and incidentally very highly priced, 'all-in-one' foods produced by the major manufacturers seem to do a satisfactory job, although the same reservations as to sources of contents, additives and preservatives apply. Many people use them with success, and the whole field of manufactured dog food has become an enormous multi-million pound industry. Basically the 'all-in-one' diets fall into three separate groups. The first, usually made in a pellet or extruded form, often known as kibbled food, consists of a mixture of meat, vegetable protein, cereals, vitamins and minerals. To the human eye and appetite, the finished product would appear to have a high 'boredom factor'. The second group of all-in-one dry foods consists of a mixture of various dried vegetable and cereal products, usually fortified with some sort of dried meat pellet. It could well be described as a rather coarse muesli. The various constituents are individually identifiable and usually contain such items as rolled grain, flaked maize, rolled dried peas etc. The quality and price of this group shows considerable variation, and in some cases the product gives the impression that it is compounded from whatever is available on the market at the time, and considerable use is made of surplus, damaged and waste products from the human food industry. The third group, usually packed in tins or air-tight plastic containers, again claims to be a complete diet, but it sets out to give the appearance of some form of meat. A typical description of the contents states: meat and animal derivatives, derivatives of vegetable origin, minerals, oils and fats. We are intrigued by the use of the word 'derivatives', and we wonder what it is about the contents that prevents them from being described simply as meat and vegetables.

In our opinion, a dog needs a mixture of meat, vegetables and cereal, and possibly additional vitamins and minerals. We therefore use one of the dry food all-in-one products as a part of the diet, plus a wholemeal biscuit or baked wholemeal bread, with added meat or tripe, the occasional cooked or fresh chopped vegetable, raw eggs – which are, after all, one of the best complete diets – and occasionally cheese. Fish is also used as an alternative to the meat content. When including eggs in the diet we crush and feed the egg shells as a source of calcium. The only supplement that we have found necessary has been sterilized bone meal as a source of calcium. For coat condition we add a small amount of margarine, vegetable oil or one the proprietary vitamin E supplements. We also have no reservations about putting almost all uneaten human food into our dog bowl and, if you are only feeding one household pet, we see no reason why such scraps should not form a considerable part of its diet, especially if used with the foods we have given and one of the complete diets.

The dog food manufacturer's nutrition experts will probably raise their hands in horror at our methods, claiming that it destroys their carefully balanced diet. However, we were raising healthy, long-lived, show-winning Rottweilers long before their products came on the market, and we have continued to do so since, making limited and sensible use of them. Furthermore, when many Rottweilers die at a relatively early age of cancer we can proudly claim that out of the many that we have owned, only two have died of this disease before the age of eleven. We like to think that this is at least partly due to the fact that we have always tried to feed our dogs on as natural a diet as possible.

All our biscuit or all-in-one alternative is soaked with hot water or gravy for an hour or so before feeding, to avoid any risk of bloat, an illness we have never had in our kennels. We do not of course soak the conventional hard dog biscuits, given as a mid-morning snack or as a treat. Our dogs are normally given one main meal a day in the evening. We like those living in kennels to go to bed with a full stomach helping them to get a good night's rest. Youngsters up to the age of eighteen months, stud dogs and in-whelp bitches receive a second meal in the morning. Each dog is fed separately, in its own dish, and the amount and content is carefully calculated for each individual. The only reason for feeding two dogs side by side – and then only under supervision – is to encourage the occasional finicky feeder who needs competition to arouse its appetite.

Chapter Six

THE ROTTWEILER
IN THE COMMUNITY

Dog lovers, and particularly those who are deeply involved in breeding and showing, tend to live in a world of their own. Nothing is more important than the next litter of puppies or the next Champion. War, economic crisis, or the rise and fall of politicians are of little interest compared with the choice of judge for the next big show, or which stud dog to use on a bitch. In the past we were able to pursue our sport and hobby with little or no interference or interest from the outside world. However, all that changed dramatically for Rottweiler owners in Britain early in 1989. The story of what happened, the resulting hate campaign against the breed, and the effect on the breed itself is currently confined to the Rottweiler in Britain, but it could happen to any breed in any country, and the warning signs must not be ignored.

The trigger for the campaign in Britain was the tragic death of an eleven-year-old girl attacked by two Rottweilers. The child was on holiday with a friend of the same age, and the two girls took the two dogs, belonging to the father of her friend, for a walk. No one will ever know what happened or why the dogs attacked. The only witness was the other child who obviously suffered a traumatic experience. Horrifying as this incident was, it is important to keep it in perspective. During 1989, when this incident occurred, there were three deaths in Britain as a result of attacks by dogs, and this was the only one involving Rottweilers. The other attacks received little or no publicity. During the ten years preceding 1989 a total of twelve people died after being bitten; none of these attacks involved Rottweilers. While it is a matter for great regret that any person should be killed by a dog, these figures should be compared with deaths from other causes such as road traffic accidents, domestic accidents, homicide, and the figure claimed by the British charity, the National Society for the Prevention of Cruelty to Children, stating that between three to four children die each week as the result of neglect or ill treatment by their parents or other people close to them. Compared with humans, the dog does not have a bad record.

However, the media were swift to seize on this isolated Rottweiler attack, and suddenly people who had owned and loved their Rottweiler for many years, found that their dog was being portrayed on radio, television and in newspapers as a monster. These owners were horrified to find that their pet dog – a member of the family, who had never given the slightest cause for complaint – was now being described as a killer and as a "devil dog". According to the media, Rottweilers were rampaging through the cities creating a reign of terror. Headlines in major national newspapers screamed "Rottweiler Terror". There were pictures of dog wardens in full protective clothing complete with riot shields under the headline "Armed for War on Killer Rottweilers", and one television news item showed a frightened black and tan mongrel being dragged half-strangled from a clump of bushes by a dog warden, accused of terrorising the neighbourhood. Its only apparent sign of aggression was to lick its tormentor's hand, but it was committing the major crime of being black and tan – the same colour as a Rottweiler. For weeks on end the media rarely allowed a day to pass without another sensational Rottweiler story. A reporter in a major national daily paper conducted an experiment. He concocted two fictitious dog-bite stories both of equal severity; one involved a Rottweiler, the other a cross-bred mongrel. He then offered the two stories to fifty newspapers. All the papers wanted the Rottweiler story, none wanted the mongrel incident.

While the media were only too happy to pontificate about the breed, their ignorance of the subject was appalling. At first we received telephone calls from newspapers asking how to spell Rottweiler, and from radio and television reporters asking how the name was pronounced. When the columnists, expressing their opinions rather than reporting news, got involved, the situation became bizarre. One very famous columnist wrote that Rottweilers attacked without warning, they did not even paw the ground, apparently confusing the Rottweiler with a bull. The failure to differentiate between bovine and canine led another reporter to state that a child had been "gored" by a Rottweiler – the "devil dog" had seemingly acquired horns. Many writers set out to convince their readers that all Rottweiler owners were moronic thugs, with less intelligence than their dogs, and suggested that the owners should be put down as well as their dogs. Repeatedly we received calls from the media asking to be put in touch with Rottweiler owners, to which we responded by offering the opportunity to interview ordinary decent owners in their own homes with their Rottweilers. Invariably these offers were refused, with the request that we find them someone whose child had been bitten by a Rottweiler. It took us something like eight months before we managed to persuade a television company to film an interview in a private house with two perfectly behaved Rottweilers.

The anti-Rottweiler campaign should be set in some sort of perspective by looking at the events which led to the attack in 1989. For almost thirty years the Rottweiler was an unqualified success. During this time the breed rose from total obscurity, unknown even to many dog experts, to one of the most popular breeds in Britain. Not only did Rottweilers attract enormous interest in the show ring, with very large entries, they were also showing their ability in working trials and as police dogs. Above all, the breed achieved a well-deserved popularity with the pet owning public. Rottweilers became a much loved part of many families. The list of owners included many famous people, but even more important were the thousands of ordinary decent people who found in the Rottweiler a faithful, loving, protective and intelligent family dog. From a mere handful in 1960 the numbers of the breed rose to about 100,000 in 1989. This popularity would not have been achieved if the breed had not shown all those qualities which the Breed Standard demands. Regrettably, success as a dog inevitably led to commercial success. Some people bred Rottweilers of poor quality, but the demand for stock was so high that they were still able to demand high prices. As a result dogs came on the market that were not only poor physical specimens, but which failed in temperament as well. However, such animals were still only a small minority. The majority of Rottweilers were excellent specimens of the breed.

The Rottweiler's dramatic rise in popularity corresponded to a general increase in the demand for pedigree dogs. Dog shows became bigger and bigger, the breeding of puppies for sale to the public became extremely profitable, and a multi-million pound supporting industry providing dog food and equipment came into existence.

The runaway success of the 'dog game' obscured the fact that far too many puppies were being produced; many of them were being discarded by their buyers when the novelty had worn off; much of the stock being bred was of poor quality and temperament, and unfit to be sold to the public. It is perhaps being charitable to say that dog people were unaware of what was happening. The money was rolling in and many were totally opposed to any action which would reduce their profits. However, there is no doubt that the blinkered approach of the majority of dog people, including the breed clubs and the Kennel Club, contributed to what was about to happen.

The growing number of dogs in Britain led to a demand that Government should introduce a dog registration scheme. The agitation for such a scheme has been led by the Royal Society for the Prevention of Cruelty to Animals on the grounds that such a scheme would reduce the number of stray dogs and assist in the control of dogs in general. This is not the place to discuss the pros and cons of dog registration. Sufficient to say that those desirous of achieving registration were prepared to spend large sums of money, using the full force of a powerful public relations department and were apparently either ignorant or indifferent to the damage that their campaign was doing to dogs and also to their own image. Dog registration has also been supported by the anti-dog lobby, who were becoming more forceful in their arguments, focusing on such matters as concern over health hazards, alleged to arise from the fouling of public places by dogs. The death of the little girl was seized on as a wonderful argument in favour of dog registration, although what difference it would have made if the dogs had been registered has never been explained.

Once the bandwagon had started to roll, everybody wanted to climb on board. Politicians, always anxious to gain publicity, jumped at the chance to express their opinion. One Member of Parliament presented a petition to Parliament asking for Rottweilers be banned and claimed 15,000 signatures in support. Smart work by a Rottweiler owner showed that these signatures had in fact been obtained on a totally different petition which, reasonably enough, called for responsible dog ownership. Two weeks after presenting the petition the M.P. had to stand up and admit that he was wrong. Another M.P. complained that he had been bitten by a Rottweiler while walking in the vicinity of the House of Commons. By a remarkable coincidence it happened on a day that the subject of dogs was being debated in the Commons. In fact, there was no certainty that the dog involved was a Rottweiler. One of the sillier sides of the whole anti-Rottweiler campaign is that virtually any large black dog becomes a Rottweiler if an incident occurs. Owners of Gordon Setters complain that they and their black and tan dogs are frequently abused by ignorant members of the public. Another group that rushed to take advantage of all the free publicity were so-called 'dog psychologists'. No newspaper article or television programme was complete without a quotation from one or more of these 'experts', usually accompanied by an attempt to advertise their services. One of the more unpleasant aspects was that these comments usually attacked the breed rather than the irresponsible owners, and it was obvious that the speakers were inclined to tell the media what they wanted to hear rather than the truth.

The anti-Rottweiler campaign created what can only be described as a state of hysteria among the general public and to a certain extent this spilled over into local government and other responsible bodies. Rottweiler owners who lived in houses which went with their jobs, such as school caretakers or golf club secretaries, were told to get rid of their dogs or lose their jobs. Building managers whose premises had in the past been used for dog shows refused to allow Rottweilers into the halls. Mothers who met their children at the school gate with the family Rottweiler were told to leave the dog at home in the future, even though the dog was perfectly behaved and enjoyed being made a fuss of by the school children. One small girl who took her school things in a grip decorated with a picture of a Rottweiler was told by her teacher to find a different bag to hold her school books. Another, whose parents owned a Rottweiler, went to her school drama class to be told by the drama teacher that the lesson for the day was for them to portray fear. To set the scene they were to imagine that there were three savage Rottweilers in the classroom. Hardly the way to instil confidence in children! There can be no doubt that, by deliberately creating a fear of Rottweilers in children and adults, the media contributed to many of the biting incidents which occurred. The mere presence of a Rottweiler was sufficient to create a state of panic, with children screaming and running. Inevitably the dog reacted and became excited, and if it was not under control, the situation rapidly deteriorated into a major incident.

Rottweilers on leads and minding their own business were frequently attacked in the streets and their owners abused. They were poisoned, shot and stabbed. Every sadistic lout considered that he had a licence to indulge in any cruelty that he chose, provided that his victim was a Rottweiler. Many dogs who had committed no offence were abandoned by their owners and the breed's welfare organisations were flooded with Rottweilers whose owners had lost confidence in a dog that had served the family happily, in some cases for many years. Litters of puppies which had suddenly become unsaleable were dumped, and even thrown out on to motorways. The very name of Rottweiler became a term of abuse. Politicians in Parliament accused each other of behaving like Rottweilers. Cartoonists used the breed to portray anything or anyone which they wished to attack, and long-running television 'soaps' included a Rottweiler incident, in order to give the subject an airing.

Comedians were delighted to find a new source of material, and 'jokes' like "What has four legs and an arm?", answer "a Rottweiler", became a typical ingredient of a cabaret act. The use of 'Rottweiler' as an insult is now a recognised part of the English language, and it would not be surprising if future dictionaries listed the word as a term of abuse.

A fact that did not help Rottweiler owners in their defence of the breed was that almost all the people whose dogs were involved in reported incidents did not give the impression that they were the type of person who would be considered a suitable owner by any serious and responsible breeder. We have already mentioned that the Rottweiler's qualities can be misused, and while the vast majority were in the hands of responsible people, a minority were used as protection by drug dealers and other criminals, as compound guards, and as a threatening weapon by young louts wanting to portray a macho image. Other owners were merely lazy or stupid, keeping Rottweilers in unfenced gardens or allowing them to run loose in public places. One of the first tasks of those defending the breed was to distance the responsible owner from such people and to make it clear that we were only too happy to see the heaviest penalties imposed on irresponsible owners.

The defence of Rottweilers also suffered from the fact that Britain has a multiplicity of breed clubs - ten, in the case of Rottweilers. While most of the clubs did their best, there were times when it would have helped to have had one strong club, capable of fighting back from a position of strength. Attempts to show that breeders were concerned and responsible by, for example, imposing a temporary ban on breeding while the overwhelmed welfare organisations tried to pick up the pieces, were defeated by those who claimed the uproar would soon disappear – they obviously worried that such a ban would affect their own money-making activities.

National Government continued to resist legislation to introduce a dog registration scheme. However, as an alternative and as a result of the adverse publicity which dogs have received, there has been an overall tightening of the legislation concerning dogs and an increase in the severity of the punishments meted out to offenders. Tough legislation against irresponsible dog owners has the support of all thinking Rottweiler owners. However, the Government has now gone beyond this by bringing in new legislation which bans certain types of dogs, such as those bred purely for fighting. The legislation names two types, the American Pit Bull Terrier and the Japanese Tosa, neither of which is recognised as a breed by the British Kennel Club. The intention of the legislation is that by banning imports, neutering existing animals and imposing other restrictions, these types will cease to exist in Britain in a few years. Similar restrictions have been brought into effect in Holland. The British legislation also allows the Government Minister concerned to bring in control orders on any breed which, in his opinion, constitutes a danger to the public. The measures that the minister can introduce are that the dog must be muzzled and on a lead in a public place. It must be admitted that there is an element of panic in this legislation as the Government is prepared to concede that it almost impossible to prove in a court of law that a dog is of a particular breed. For instance, how do you prove that a particular dog is a Rottweiler and not a fat Dobermann or a large black-and-tan mongrel? And how would you categorise a cross-breed? It is ironical that the owners who would suffer under such legislation are those who had registered their dogs at the Kennel Club, and who could not, therefore, dispute what breed it was. There can be no doubt that if Rottweiler breeders had not risen in vigorous defence of their breed, it would almost certainly have been added to the banned list, and there will always be a grave risk of it being made the subject of special controls.

Writing two years after the anti Rottweiler campaign started, it is possible to see the effect it has had on the breed. The numbers of dogs that have been thrown out of their homes and have either been abandoned or destroyed cannot be calculated – the figure almost certainly runs into thousands. Some indication can be obtained from the numbers handled by the Rottweiler Welfare organisation, but these only represent a small percentage of the total. In the ten years between 1978 and 1987 a total of 136 dogs needed their help. In the following two years the figure was in excess of 700, and this does not include those dogs which Welfare was unable to help because of shortage of kennel space and lack of funds. It became virtually impossible to rehome unwanted Rottweilers, and Welfare was forced to advise many of the applicants that the only course open to them was to put their dog down. A similar picture can be obtained from the English Kennel Club registration figures, which tend to run about six months in arrears. For a number of years the registration figures for Rottweilers were in the region of 2,500 per quarter or 10,000 per year. By the second quarter of 1990 the figure had dropped to 909 and by the third quarter to 710 – a reduction in a year of almost two-thirds. The market for puppies has virtually disappeared, and puppy purchasers are limited to those have owned the breed before and have not lost sight of its virtues.

At this moment in time, it would appear that the situation we have been describing is virtually confined to Britain. However, other countries have shown similar trends, with campaigns to ban certain breeds or to place special restrictions on them. A recent article in an American magazine, which had no connection with dogs, quotes the writer as saying he did not like the district that he was living in "because the next house had two Rottweilers in the back yard, a sure sign that drug dealers were in the neighbourhood" – yet another indication that the breed is being misused, and acquiring a bad name. Looking at the reasonably steady registration figures for

Rottweilers in other European countries and comparing them with the enormous increases in Britain and the U.S.A. over the last twenty years, it is obvious that this was a bubble that had to burst. What has happened to the Rottweiler in Britain can only be described as a tragedy, but it may in the long term be beneficial. The financial incentive to breed large quantities of stock, some of which was of poor quality, has disappeared. It is to be hoped that the breed can go forward into the future, much reduced in numbers, but in the hands of people who love and understand it.

Chapter Seven

THE ROTTWEILER
AT WORK

The Rottweiler is a highly intelligent breed and is capable of carrying out the wide variety of tasks which man asks of it. This ranges from highly skilled work in the police and armed forces, to general farm work, competing in Working Trials, Obedience and Agility competitions, and in the relatively new role as a therapeutic aid to the sick. It is is also superb in performing the duties of a house dog and family pet, which is, after all, the function of the vast majority of Rottweilers.

While many European countries and the U.S.A. use a variety of breeds, including the Rottweiler, for work with the police and armed forces, the breed most commonly used in Britain is the German Shepherd Dog. This is for a number of reasons and does not necessarily mean that the GSD is considered better for the job. Firstly, most people involved are GSD-orientated, having worked with them for many years. Secondly, these services largely rely on being given dogs that are unwanted by their owners or can be purchased at a very low price. The large numbers of GSDs in

Britain means that there are many such dogs to choose from, even though the reject rate is high. Thirdly, the training of a Rottweiler requires an able and patient handler, qualities which are not as essential in the training of a GSD. Finally, for civil police work, the power and biting ability of a Rottweiler can be a disadvantage in some circumstances, especially if this factor is not understood by those controlling the use of the dog.

A number of Rottweilers have been used by the police in Britain, and these dogs have usually achieved an excellent reputation during their careers. On each occasion they have been trained and subsequently handled by someone who has combined both respect and understanding of the breed with long experience of police dog training in general. In many cases the handler has been so determined to work a Rottweiler that he has bought and reared his own puppy until it was old enough to be taken on the strength as a police dog. Most of these handlers will agree that the Rottweiler took longer to learn and required more careful handling, but they will also agree that the end product was superior to the majority of GSDs, and well worth the extra effort.

The first British police officer to train and work a Rottweiler was Roy Hunter. After he retired as a police inspector he went on to build an international career, both in Britain and the U.S.A. as a trainer of both dogs and owners. This is his story in his own words:

"I was fortunate in being allowed to handle and train Abelard of Mallion, who was one of the first litter of Rottweilers to be born in this country. Compared to my previous police dog, a GSD gift dog from a back street in North London, Abelard was like a Rolls Royce compared to an old banger. His tracking was superb, his chasing was firm; no one could ever shake him, let alone shake him off, as he was so big and powerful. His searching, whether for a large human, or a tiny article was 100 per cent reliable. Luckily, considering his size and strength, his temperament was steady. He would not attack another dog without provocation – and not even then, unless I was unaware of the incident. He would not attack a human without my command. He was absolutely under control. Together we averaged thirty arrests a year, a figure which exceeded the total achieved by all the other dogs and handlers on the division. As a result of this we were twice recommended for the Black Knight Trophy which was awarded to the most outstanding team in the Dog Section. We were also in the Metropolitan Police Dog Demonstration Team."

Proof that Abelard had working ability bred into him can be seen in the fact that a full brother of his from a later litter, Bruin of Mallion, became the first Rottweiler

Working Trials Champion in Britain. However, it takes two to make a team, and Roy certainly showed that he knew how to get the most out of a Rottweiler. He goes on to describe his first operation.

"The first job I had with Abby was after we had been out of training school about a week. A stolen car had been abandoned out in the sticks at Enfield. An area car took us to the scene. The officers already there assured me that no one had been near the car. I took Abby up to the driver's seat, let him sniff around to impress the onlookers, and then I put his harness on and let him sniff the ground around the driver's door where the actual track would start. He sniffed a few times, and then started off towards some barns. I kept pressure on the tracking line and followed behind him. He went round a corner before me. I heard a kerfuffle and ran around the corner to find Abelard the proud possessor of a Mallard duck! I got the duck from his mouth unharmed, but his incentive to track had gone. So had my credibility – all the cops were rolling about laughing!"

Neither Roy nor Abby had long to wait before they had a chance to restore their reputation. This was another tracking operation.

"Two days later we were called to a truck parked 200 yards from an old flooded quarry. By the truck was a pile of clothes, and the driver had not been seen for four hours. The local police wanted proof that the driver was in the water before they would call out the Thames Division boats to search for him. Again, I let Abby sniff the ground around the clothes, then he tracked in a straight line to the water. The river police were called and the body was recovered."

Most police officers who have handled Rottweilers will tell you that when a dog was required to carry out a particularly difficult track, it was usually a case of "Send for the Rottweiler". The next task for Roy and Abby involved tracking and a search.

"I was called to a house that was occupied by villains. An observant officer had seen signs on the pavement where a safe had been dragged across into the house. He called for back-up and a dog. When I knocked at the door I was greeted by a slovenly woman who said: "Where's your warrant?", embroidering her question with a number of four-letter words. I replied: "Here he is," pointing in a way which was a signal to Abby to speak. Abby obliged, the woman stood well back and I went through the house into the garden, other officers remaining at the house. I took Abby's lead off and told him "find". He leapt over two fences, and within seconds of going through the house, he was barking at a garden shed two gardens away – this was my first crime arrest with Abby. By the way, the safe contained £307, and my Divisional Number, the number cops wear on their shoulder, was, wait for it – yes, 307Y!"

Work for Roy Hunter and Abby covered all sorts of tasks and took them to many different places.

"One week in every three months we were on loan to 'C' Division which covered the West End of London, including Soho. Two dogs and their handlers patrolled together. Once Abby was seen, the streets were cleared – and that is no exaggeration. We would walk along one street, with a dog and handler on each pavement and then return up another, constantly keeping the crowds moving. Soho was bad in the early sixties."

Like many dogs, Abby suffered from flatulence. As a result, Roy claims that he could clear a crowded bar or club without even barking. The same attribute could cause four burly policemen to evacuate a police car! The physical strength and power of the Rottweiler is well illustrated by Roy's next story.

"My first chase came in the West End. We were standing near Leicester Square when an excited member of the public ran up and said a robbery was in progress at a nearby restaurant. I ran through the front doors of the restaurant, along with another cop. Fortunately, the restaurant had just closed, so there were no customers, but the cashier was on the floor with blood coming from a wound in her head. I told the other officer to stay with her and to get assistance, and I ran through the back doors. A black man waving a pick-axe handle was running towards me, chased by a soldier in uniform. I shouted to the squaddy to stand still and released Abby. The suspect turned and ran the other way, and was taken to the ground by 102lbs. of Rottweiler. I ran up and secured him until help arrived. This incident was reported in the national Press, but no two newspapers told the same story."

On another occasion Abby showed that he was intelligent enough to make his own assessment of a situation, and showed that he was prepared to attack without a command, in order to protect his handler.

"One particularly busy night in Tottenham, I was in a car with two other cops and Abelard, when we passed a crowd in a shop doorway. They were milling around fighting, and obviously drunk. As a drunk can be a nuisance with a police dog, I left Abby in the car as we went across to separate them. I was restraining one man when I heard a yell behind me, and another man hurtled on to my back with Abby hanging on to his right arm. In the man's right hand was the starting-handle of a car. Abby had seen what was about to happen. He had squeezed out of the half-opened window, run across the road, and saved me from getting my head smashed in."

Roy describes these incidents as typical of the work of a police dog.

"Crowd control with a dog like Abby was always a doddle. All he had to do was bark, and the crowd froze. He was also gentle with kids. If we had an open day at a police station, the kids were attracted to him straightaway, and he loved their attention."

This comment about Abby's behaviour with children is particularly significant, bearing in mind that he was obviously a very tough dog. It illustrates how the apparently conflicting requirements of good nature and toughness, required by the Standard, can come together. Roy Hunter stresses the point that you need a special kind of handler to get the best out of a Rott, and such a handler should be physically active, to ensure that his Rottweiler remains fit. He also suggests, and we agree with him, that many Rotts can become overweight and lazy, given half a chance. He emphasises that the Rottweiler needs to be worked and have his brain used in order to develop and maintain its potential. He makes one final, but important point: "Rotts with aggressive, excitable or 'macho' handlers are likely to develop the same characteristics."

Abelard of Mallion retired from the police force at seven years of age. Sadly, he died the day after he ceased to be on duty. One can only wonder whether this was coincidence, or did this tough old warrior decide that life without his regular "rumble" while on duty, would be too boring?

In the sixties and early seventies there were between six and ten Rottweilers working with the British police. Today, as far as we know, there are none. Many of the reasons for this can be attributed to cost, suitability of handlers, and time required for training. Although the dogs used in the sixties performed well and some of them were outstanding, the sheer power and biting ability of the Rottweiler was a disadvantage as far as civil police work was concerned. All too often, a senior officer would order a dog to be used against the advice of the handler. When, as a result, excessive injury was caused, the dog took the blame. On more than one occasion, a police Rottweiler was destroyed for doing the job for which it had been

Police Constable Robert Pike with Police Dog 'Tarka'.   *Eastern Evening News.*

trained. It has been said, and there is some truth in the remark, that it is not a question of whether the Rottweiler is good enough for the police but rather, whether the police are good enough for the Rottweiler.

The failure of the Rottweiler to fulfil its early promise, both as a police dog and in Working Trials cannot really be blamed on the dog. While we admit that the breed was perhaps too tough for work as a civilian police dog, the failure, as we have already said, was one of human management rather than the fault of the dog. Initially, the interest of police handlers was aroused by the introduction of a new breed and a desire to find out what it could do. Handlers like Roy Hunter and a number of others took up the challenge and, like Roy, showed that the breed had a lot to offer. However, once the novelty began to wear off, the difficulties began to outweigh the benefits, and the police lost interest. After all, the GSD could do all that was required, so why make life difficult by using a breed that was more difficult to train and obtain?

The courage and power of the Rottweiler have, however, continued to attract handlers who are not required to act under the same restraints as the civil police, and

A British Army Rottweiler having his daily grooming. Service dogs are taught to wear a muzzle for a fixed period each day.   *J. Cunningham.*

A British Army Rottweiler demonstrates his tracking skills.   *J. Cunningham.*

so these qualities have proved to be an advantage. The British Army has used a number of Rottweilers and continues to do so, although they represent a small percentage of the total number of dogs used by the Army. To quote the officer in charge of Army dog training: "All Rottweilers in Army service fully meet the high standard of obedience and performance required for their work. Most are used as protection dogs: patrolling an area with their handler and capable of indicating the presence of an intruder, pursuing and holding the intruder on command, and protecting its handler if he is attacked." The same source makes the point that the Rottweiler is capable not only of achieving a high standard of obedience, but also of tolerating a change of handler. The willingness to accept a change of handler may come as a surprise to many Rottweiler owners, although we have always found it to be the case, given time and understanding. The Army also comments that, as protection dogs, they are undoubtedly of great deterrent value – an aspect of the Rottweiler's character which has not always worked to the breed's advantage. A senior Army dog trainer said: "When Rottweilers are good, they are very good; when they are bad, they are awful." A sentiment that many of us would agree with.

The Army also uses Rottweilers for more advanced work such as tracking and scene-of-crime searches. It has long been rumoured that there are Rottweilers working with the Special Air Service, but the S.A.S. does not discuss its work, and no confirmation of this or further details are available. Probably the most famous

Handlers must be skilful to get the best from a Rottweiler, and this senior Army instructor is responsible for training men and dogs in the advanced work that is required.   *J. Cunningham.*

Rottweilers of the Austrian Army Display Team.

group of Rottweilers serving man in relatively large numbers are those with the Austrian Army dog section, which uses far more Rotts than any other breed. They are well aware of the value of publicity and a demonstration by one of their teams is a spectacle well worth seeing. Much of the credit for the success of the Austrian Army Rottweilers must go to someone who is without doubt one of the greatest living experts on the breed, Herr Adolf Ringer, civilian head and chief trainer of the school.

Having discussed the Rottweiler working for man in circumstances where its strength and courage are called for, it is perhaps appropriate to look at a different task, one which requires the gentle and affectionate side of the Rottweiler's temperament. Man's association and mutual friendship with the dog goes back into the mists of history. It has long been recognised that the affection of a dog can have a therapeutic effect on many humans. Quite apart from those many fit and well people who gain enormous pleasure from their dog, this association can be beneficial to those who, for reasons of infirmity, old age or general circumstances, are unable to keep a dog as their personal pet. A number of organisations have been formed to fill this need, selecting and training dogs for the purpose of visiting patients in hospitals, in old people's homes and similar institutions. The function of these dogs has been to provide a regular service whereby people can talk to the dogs, cuddle them, and enjoy their companionship for a short while. Any dog lover who has been deprived of the company of their pet for a period will understand the pleasure which such a visit can bring. The major organisation in Britain for this purpose has been set up under the auspices of the Pro-Dogs National Charity, which works to further the cause of dogs. Pro-Dogs coined the descriptive title of 'P.A.T. Dogs' for this work, from the name Pro-Dogs Active Therapy, and for convenience we will use this term, although other organisations, such as Canine Concern, are doing equally effective work under other names. In the U.S.A., where they are known as Therapy Dogs, there are many Rottweilers doing this wonderful work. As with the description of a working police Rottweiler, we will use the experiences of one Rottweiler and its handler as a typical example, allowing the handler to tell his story in his own words. It is a story that not only shows the happiness that such a dog can bring to many people, but also how a dog can suffer pain and discomfort, yet still retain a loving and gentle nature. Nigel Tombling bought Holly, his P.A.T. dog, with the intention of showing her, but he did not have a lot of luck with her in this capacity. However, this did not stop him from giving her the love and care she deserved, and he helped her to play a very useful part in the community. Here is his story.

"Holly was born on November 16th 1986, and was bought by us to be a show dog. We already had a dog from the same breeder, which we were showing at open show level. At an early age it was obvious that Holly was not going to be a show dog, as her mouth was going to be undershot. However, we did not have the heart to part with her as she had such a lovely temperament, and so we decided to keep her as a pet. In mid-1987 we noticed that she was starting to develop lameness in her rear legs and she showed a tendency to take most of her weight on her front legs. Our vet took X-rays which indicated osteochondritis dissecans (OCD) in both hocks. As a result, Holly had an operation on her right hock, which was the worst one, at Cambridge University. This was in October 1987 when she was ten and a half months old. We knew the post-operative treatment that was involved, as our other dog had been operated on for OCD in the elbow earlier in the year. Holly was spayed in January 1988, and at the same time her hips were X-rayed for Hip Dysplasia and further X-rays of her hocks were taken. The hock X-rays showed developing degenerative joint disease: both hocks were swollen with very little movement in them."

Obviously Holly had a lot of trouble, and many owners would have given up and decided that the kindest thing would be for her to be put to sleep. However, Nigel obviously felt that if Holly was determined to make the best of it, it was up to him to give her all the help that he could.

"Holly was taking all these problems completely in her stride, and it was not affecting her temperament in the slightest. She was still the biggest softie, and loving everybody to death. I must admit that in her first year of life I always seemed to be taking her to the vet, and I did wonder about her life expectancy with two bad back legs."

Even if Holly was to have a short life, Nigel wanted her to have an interesting one. "She was good at her obedience classes but could not sit straight because of her hocks, and everything that she did took that little bit longer. I decided that, as she loved everybody, I would give her a try on the P.A.T. dog scheme. I filled in the forms, and my vet carried out the assessment. I am happy to say that she was accepted in May 1988."

Holly and Nigel made their first trip with an experienced P.A.T. dog visitor.

"We went along to an old people's residential home run by the local authority. If the first trip was successful, we would continue to visit it on a regular basis. We went in with Holly on her lead, and I wondered how she would cope, as she had never experienced anything like it before. I need not have worried – she took to it like a duck to water. She soon knew that she had to go to each chair to see each person and have a fuss made of her, if required. It did not concern her in the slightest if the patting was sometimes a bit hard, or if it was not co-ordinated properly, or if she was poked in the face at the same time. She loved everybody that she met and would give them a big wet kiss, given half a chance."

Holly's probationary visit was a success and she became a regular P.A.T. dog visitor.

"I had to watch the amount of sweets and titbits which everybody wanted to give her, as I was worried about her carrying excess weight. In fact, if she is given a sweet during her visits she takes it politely, but immediately spits it out – a bit embarrassing to say the least! Perhaps she has decided that she should not eat on duty, as at home any titbit is gone in a flash. She had to get used to travelling in the lift, which took us up to the first floor. The alternative was a flight of rather steep stairs, and I was worried about those legs of hers. The first time she did not quite

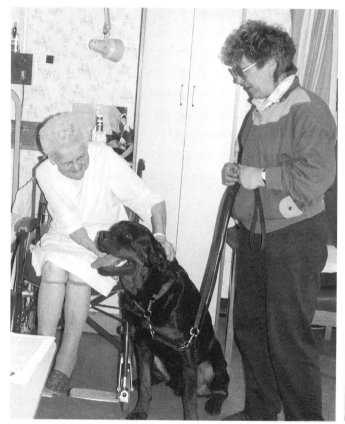

Patients look forward to visits from therapy dogs, and some will make special friends with a particular dog.

A Rottweiler P.A.T. dog shows how calm and steady this breed can be when required.

know what was happening, but now she loves it and does not even consider using the stairs."

Holly continued her visits, becoming more at home as the routine became familiar.

"After several visits with Holly on the lead, I decided I would try her off the lead, as it could become a little complicated with the lead becoming entangled with chairs and walking-frames. I had no need to worry. Typically, Holly does the job just the same. She now knows the routine so well that I could just stand at the front door and let her carry on, on her own. She knows that we visit the office first to announce our arrival, then we go to each of the four lounges, always in the same sequence, and then up in the lift to the first floor. The only thing she has not learnt to do is operate the lift!"

The gentle side of a Rottweiler character comes to the fore in therapy work.

Holly has made herself extremely popular, not only with the patients but with the staff, although there was the odd exception.

"All the staff love Holly, although the majority did not know what a Rottweiler was when she first went there. I had a scare one day, after we had been visiting a few times. We were in the hall going from one lounge to the next when a female staff member came out of the dining room, took one look at Holly, screamed the place down and fled, slamming the door behind her. Holly could not make out what was wrong! It turned out that this particular lady was petrified of all dogs and we had not met her before. She still runs and hides when she sees Holly, but Holly pretends not to notice."

A year after Holly started her visits the anti-Rottweiler publicity started. Many hospitals and old people's homes were so influenced by the outrageous allegations made about Rottweilers in the media that they stopped allowing Rottweilers to visit under the P.A.T. dog scheme, even though the particular dogs had been visiting for years without giving the slightest cause for alarm.

To protect themselves Pro-Dogs had to introduce a scheme whereby Rottweiler owners had to obtain a certificate from the institution to the effect that they were willing to accept a Rottweiler P.A.T. dog. Fortunately, Holly was far too popular for this to cause any trouble.

"The staff were very good, and their attitude towards Holly did not change in the slightest. She has even converted some of the visitors she meets when making her rounds. As far as the residents are concerned, the majority of them look upon Holly as a big black dog, with no tail, who comes to visit them. The few who do know what a Rottweiler is are very proud that they have this big friendly one who comes to see them."

The very real benefit that visits from a dog like Holly can give are illustrated by seemingly unimportant events.

"A nurse told me about a woman resident who was always very keen to meet Holly. We always had the same conversation. She would tell me that Holly was "a big dog", a "good boy!", she had "clean teeth, and a nice coat", and that she must "take a lot of feeding". Apparently, this woman scarcely ever spoke, except when Holly was there. Yet, in Holly's company she relaxed and, for a short time, was happy in the companionship of the dog. It gives me a very proud feeling to see the good that Holly is doing in a case like this."

Obviously, in an old people's home residents die, and there were times when Holly would find an empty chair.

"Holly takes it in her stride. She will go up to the chair and if it is empty, pass on to the next. However, Holly always remembers one resident who is no longer there, or more accurately she remembers a patch of wall above the chair this lady sat in. When we first went to the home this particular lady had a cut-out of a cat in black felt stuck to the wall above her chair. From day one, Holly was absolutely fascinated by this felt cat; she was always staring at it, and even to this day she goes to the same chair to look at the spot where the cat used to be. The home does have one resident who absolutely hates Holly's visits. This is a large tabby tom-cat. Holly ignores him, except to stare fixedly, which is the signal for him to disappear. Then Holly eats his dish of food and milk!"

Nigel Tombling persuaded the local Press to do an article about Holly's work and she was photographed for the paper in September 1988. However, they were not interested in highlighting her work when the anti-Rottweiler campaign started in 1989. This was a wonderful example of a Rottweiler doing a magnificent job in the community – and yet Nigel met with a point-blank refusal when he asked the Press to publicise the good side of the breed. Holly sets a wonderful example for the breed. The pain and discomfort that she has suffered has in no way affected the love and affection that she shows, not only for her owner but for humans in general. Thankfully, there are many Rottweilers like her, but not all of them have had the help and love that Nigel and his wife have given their dog. The last words on Holly come from Nigel:

"Holly is now just over four years old, and she copes with her hock problems very well. She has no treatment or medication, and the only time that she is stiff on her legs is if she does too much running around and playing. She can move very fast if she wants to. Obviously, she has developed a very well-built front end compared to her rear end. At home Holly is No. 1 bitch; we have three other bitches and she keeps them all in their place. She loves a cuddle and likes nothing more than sitting on my lap where she will happily go off to sleep and snore the place down!"

Rottweiler lovers owe much to people like Nigel Tombling, who works hard with little thanks or publicity for his efforts. He does more for the good name of the breed than all the much publicised show winners, and this goes a long way towards refuting the ignorant attacks on the breed. The use of dogs to help people in this way has been described as "tail-wagging psychotherapy", and we are delighted that Rottweilers are able to play their part in this work.

Many Rottweilers work for their living as farm dogs, herding cattle and sheep, often riding with their master in the back of a pick-up truck or even on a platform on the back of a three-wheeled motorcycle. We know of one Rott who flies with its owner in his private plane. Many more earn their keep as well as the gratitude of their owners by accompanying them on lonely journeys, acting as both companion and protector. Helga, owned by Tracy St Clair Pearce is a Rottweiler that combines farm work with therapy work. The farm includes Shetland sheep, rare Shetland cattle and Shetland ducks, as well as turkeys and Angora rabbits. Helga regularly herds the sheep and cows, and is quite prepared to tackle the same job with the rest of the stock. The fence enclosing the rabbits is only two feet in height, but she never attempts to jump it, remaining an interested spectator. Her record with sheep was when she brought in a flock of two hundred and fifty ewe lambs, which she

Rottweiler working enthusiasts – five of these dogs are qualified to CD ex. standard.

controlled while one wayward ram lamb was removed. The only creature she was defeated by was a thirty-pound stag turkey, named Ethelred. This bird was convinced, quite unfairly, that Helga was responsible for the death of his much-loved hen, Cutie Pie. He would attack Helga on sight, and the regular routine was a chase around the car parked in the yard, until Helga found the opportunity to make a dash for the house door. Although she passed her P.A.T. tests with flying colours, Helga visits old people in their homes. One of her patients is a seventy-two year old man, who suffers from Parkinson's disease. For the first two visits he completely ignored Helga, so on the third visit she was left at home. Immediately he wanted to know what was wrong: was the dog ill? Didn't she like him? From then on, they became firm friends, although following all the anti-Rottweiler feeling, he now tells his relatives that he is visited by a lovely German Shepherd Dog! In the village all the old people know Helga, and if anyone dares to criticise the breed, they all leap to its defence.

When the Rottweiler first became established in Britain, many of us hoped that its working ability would result in the breed making a major impact on the sport of Working Trials. Initially this did happen. Long before the breed was allocated Challenge Certificates in the show ring, there were two Rottweilers with the title of Working Trials Champion. A number of others also achieved considerable success. However, while Rottweilers have continued to work in Obedience, Agility and Working Trials, their numbers have been relatively few compared with the total number of the breed registered with the Kennel Club. There are probably several

The heavily-built Rottweiler is a surprisingly agile dog for its weight.

reasons for this. Firstly, the breed's versatility has meant that while it can do many tasks, it excels at only a few of them. A classic example of "Jack of all trades, master of none", Rottweilers are perhaps too heavy for the scale and jumps, too thick-set for some of the agility exercises, not precise enough for some heelwork. They can do all these things and do them well, but not with the mechanical perfection of some of the other breeds. However, the Rottweiler is supreme at tracking and at man-work, and when it comes to sheer courage and determination, no other breed can equal it. Success in this type of competition can be considered in two ways: success with a particular breed overcoming all the problems that arise from that breed, such as agility and body shape; or success in competition irrespective of breed, in which case you choose the dog most suitable for your purpose. To many people the most important thing is to win, and the selection of what breed to use is made on this criterion alone. Thankfully, there are still people who wish to work with the Rottweiler, and we can only hope that this band of enthusiasts will continue and perhaps increase in numbers.

Finally we come to the biggest group of Rottweilers who serve mankind as

Retrieving a dumb-bell over the 'A' Frame.

companions and much-loved pets. Probably 90 per cent of all the puppies produced in Britain and the U.S.A. go into pet homes, and it is the behaviour of these dogs which makes or mars the breed's reputation. Many of these Rottweilers do some of the other tasks we have been discussing, but they are primarily housedogs, companions and pets. If proof is needed of the success of the Rottweiler as a family dog, we have only to look at the enormous number of Rotts who live with a family, and the fact that when such a dog dies of old age, the only acceptable replacement is another Rottweiler. We have lost count of the number of heartbroken owners who have telephoned us to say that their wonderful old dog has died, and they must have another Rottweiler. The people who have lived with a Rottweiler for many years cannot believe that any other breed could ever be as intelligent, faithful and loving as a Rott. A glance at any American Rottweiler publication will feature numerous photographs and anecdotes of Rottweilers playing their part in the lives of their families: playing with children, enjoying the beach, back-packing in the mountains –

Billy McWilliam and his Rottweiler, Bamber Rastus, represented Scotland at Crufts from 1985 to 1990, and at the Dublin Horse of the Year Show.   *Alan V. Walker.*

Children are encouraged to learn more about dogs as part of a holiday play scheme.
with the family Rottweiler carrying its own ruck-sack of supplies – or just lying in
front of a fire.

Stories of the Rottweiler as a member of the family tend to reflect the breed's
affectionate gentle nature, as opposed to its toughness, although this does not mean
that it will not display this harder side, if his family need it. There can be no doubt
that many a family have escaped attack, burglary, or even worse, because of the
deterrent presence of the family Rottweiler. We have always found that our own
dogs took their cue from the tone of our voice. A friendly greeting to a visitor
produced the same response in our dogs. However, the slightest inference that
implied that the visitor was not welcome meant that they became alert and watchful.
Sybil and Ron Harper, who have owned Rottweilers as family pets for many years,
tell a story which illustrates this aspect of the breed:

"This tale goes back to the early sixties when party gate-crashing and drugs
seemed to be the norm. We had read about these things, but we did not dream that it
could happen literally on our own doorstep. Our eldest son asked if he could have a

Rottweilers are very adaptable, and enjoy the challenge of learning a new task.

party for his friends and their girlfriends. We agreed, as long as we could stay around. We had a study at the end of the house and decided to spend the evening there, well stocked with refreshments, radio and books. We also had our two Rottweiler bitches, one large three-year-old and a fairly hefty nine-month-old puppy. We had spent the day preparing loads of food, a large bowl of mild punch and assorted cans and bottles. The party started and we withdrew to our room. Everything seemed to be going according to plan. Lots of laughter and loud thumping music. Suddenly our son came into our room looking very worried and said: "We have been invaded." He explained that the last guest had seen a van pulling up behind him, and had left the door open thinking more guests were arriving. However, the last lot were uninvited. We suggested that he should try to solve the problem himself, but we felt that we should be ready to offer some back-up. We heard him turn the music off and say: "This is a private party, please leave." This obviously had no effect. We then went into the room to find that the invaders consisted of some thirty to forty hippies, who having already eaten all the food and drunk all the drink, were now sitting around smoking pot and asking our son for more. Ordering them out still had no effect, so the two Rottweilers were brought in on leads. The mere sight and sound of the dogs was sufficient to clear the room.

Peace was restored; the party was resupplied and restarted. At the end of the party, the two dogs enjoyed being made a fuss of by the legitimate guests. What is significant is that the same gang gate-crashed another nearby party later that evening. Lacking a pair of Rottweilers, the householder finished up in hospital, and the house was badly damaged."

Many breed clubs hold events which are designed to be fun for both dogs and owners. A popular event at many of them is a fancy dress parade. While your initial reaction to Rottweilers being dressed up in funny clothes may be one of disapproval, it would appear that most Rotts enjoy being the centre of attraction in this way, and are neither frightened nor annoyed by wearing funny hats or frilly knickers. We have seen Micky and Minnie Mouse, Police Constable Plod complete with truncheon, and many others. All the Rottweiler performers seemed to enjoy themselves, especially if the prizes they won were edible. The Harpers dressed their pair up as a backward pupil complete with school satchel and dunce cap, and teacher wearing mortar board and holding her cane in her teeth.

The gentleness of the breed shows itself in surprising ways. Another dog owned by the Harpers, named Samson, loved to swim. His favourite pool was a nearby reservoir which contained a considerable amount of floating debris, some of which he always insisted on retrieving. His biggest catch was a large wooden door, but his most intriguing was a large pike. When this was taken from his mouth and returned to the water, it swam away unharmed – although probably a little shocked. Our own Dutch import, Luther, used his mouth very gently. On one occasion he was in a wool shop, and he carefully inspected a large display pyramid of balls of wool. The one he wanted was almost at the bottom of the pile. With infinite care he removed the chosen ball. You can hardly blame him for not understanding that this resulted in the complete collapse of the entire display! On another occasion he decided that he would like the sock that was being worn by a baby in a pram outside a shop. Very gently, he took hold of the sock and slid it off the baby's foot. The child thought it was highly amusing, and fortunately so did the child's mother. Although on each occasion he was proud of the treasure that he had acquired, he was quite willing to return it when told to do so. Luther, who lived in the house, had as a companion an extremely bossy Yorkshire Terrier. Most of the time he would ignore being attacked and sworn at by the Yorkie. Whatever the provocation, he would never growl or snap. However, he had one very effective way of solving the problem. When the Yorkie became too insufferable Luther would pin him gently to the floor with one paw, holding him there until the Yorkie had, at least for a short time, learnt to behave. When the owners of Rottweiler family dogs talk about their pets, there are always two aspects of the dog's character which are mentioned – the Rottweiler's sense of humour, and the fact that they are "characters". To be honest, while the Rott may be happy to laugh with you and at you, it is not, in our opinion, so happy to be laughed at. Certainly Luther would develop a very cold stare and walk off in a huff if he considered that you were laughing at him, especially if your merriment involved a loss of dignity on his part. On the other hand, James has a highly developed sense of fun and will play the clown with the deliberate intention of making his audience laugh, spurred on to greater efforts by applause. This is a technique he has used to great advantage as a stud dog – human females are not the only ones who are more easily seduced by a sense of fun and humour!

One of our early Rottweilers, Gunther, went to Jersey where he lived a luxurious life in a household that did a lot of entertaining. He had a number of party tricks, two of which involved dinner parties. He could open all the bedroom doors, and as soon as everyone had settled at the dinner table he would do a tour of the bedrooms collecting items of female underwear. He would then take these downstairs to the dining room where he would deposit his collection in the lap of the master of the house, who then had the embarrassing task of identifying and returning these items to the various lady guests. His second trick was to lie under the dining table with the aim of stealing the guest's table napkins. He was very quiet about it, gently sliding it from your lap so that you probably did not know that it had gone. Once stolen, he would proceed to reduce the napkin to shreds. The host considered that it was reasonable for you to lose one napkin, but to lose a second was a social gaffe.

Stories of pet Rottweilers could fill a book of their own. Suffice to say that it is the ability to form part of the family, coupled with his other characteristics, that have made the Rottweiler so immensely popular with the public. It is only by ensuring that these aspects are not lost that we can ensure that this breed retains its rightful place in the community.

Ch. Lana's Lass of Chesara: everything a Rottweiler should be, and still feminine.
                                                                                    Pearce

Chapter Eight

THE BREED STANDARD

This chapter sets out to detail and discuss the Breed Standards drawn up for the Rottweiler. Although there is only one Rottweiler and all Standards describe the same dog, there are in fact three Breed Standards currently in use in the world. Firstly there is the F.C.I. Standard, which is the German Standard as approved by the ADRK, secondly there is the American Standard and thirdly the British. They vary in the amount of detailed description included, and in phraseology. With the exception of a few items in the ADRK Standard, the actual requirements as to the physical description of the dog do not differ between the three. However, there are very good reasons for looking at all three Standards. The ADRK Standard has to be accepted as the prime source for anyone studying the breed. It is the basis on which both the American and British Standards were originally written, and both countries set out to produce what was, in fact, the ADRK Standard written in English. When you look at the ADRK Standard, it is important to be aware that the Germans use their Standard as a regulator, and as a result they make amendments from time to time, with the aim of correcting faults which may have become apparent as the breed develops. In the U.S.A and in Britain we tend to consider that a Breed Standard is written on tablets of stone, describing the ideal dog, and that it should not be altered except for extremely good reasons. In fact, a criticism that is sometimes made in the U.K. is that breeders try and change the Standard, or, at least, its interpretation, to fit the dogs that they have produced, rather than producing a dog to fit the Standard. The American Standard is of importance firstly because of its quality, and because in its illustrated form – produced by the American Rottweiler Club – it offers any student of the breed a large number of extremely useful illustrations as an aid to understanding; secondly it is the Standard for the country which has the largest Rottweiler population in the world. The British Standard is used throughout the English-speaking world, with the exception of North America. We were very much involved in the production of the first British Breed Standard issued in 1965, and we make no secret of the fact that we consider that the 1986 revision to be a poor shadow of the original. The British Kennel Club, having been given a remit to standardise main headings and terminology, went much further and, in our opinion, reduced the Standards of many breeds from a warm-hearted portrait compiled by people who knew and loved their dogs to a cold-blooded blueprint.

When a Breed Standard is applied in the show ring by a judge, it becomes a matter of how that judge interprets its requirements. It is not possible to reduce a living creature to a precise collection of geometrical shapes, angles, proportions and colour graduations. Furthermore, after the various detailed aspects have been considered, the final decision must be made on the overall appearance of the dog: its balance and its ability to carry out its function. The bottom line will always be the judge's personal opinion based, we hope, on the Breed Standard. It will also include, to a certain extent, a judge's personal feelings on the weight to be given to a particular aspect. Some judges consider heads to be of vital importance, others will look for good movement, others will feel that some other aspect is of major importance. There is nothing wrong with these differences of opinion between judges. Collectively they help to ensure that no one aspect or fault of the breed is given undue prominence, and if all judges were of the same opinion there would be no more dog shows – the same dog would win all the time.

We propose to discuss the Breed Standards by quoting the relevant section from each, followed by our comments. To do this it has been necessary to rearrange the order in some cases, but all parts of the Standards are included. The Standards used are the latest available at the time of writing: the ADRK 1988, the AKC 1990, and the U.K. 1988. The line illustrations are from *The ARC Illustrated Standard*. We are extremely grateful for permission to include these most excellent drawings.

Heady study: Ch. Gbos Gaytimes, winner of 14 CCs and 9 RCCs. Owned by Mrs H. Wilson.

Pearce.

GENERAL APPEARANCE

ADRK: The Rottweiler is a medium-large, robust dog neither gross nor slight, nor spindly. In correct proportion he is compactly and powerfully built indicating great strength, manoeuvrability and endurance.

AKC: The ideal Rottweiler is a medium large, robust and powerful dog with clearly defined rust markings. His compact and substantial build denotes great strength, agility and endurance. Dogs are characteristically more massive throughout with larger frame and heavier bone than bitches. Bitches are distinctly feminine, but without weakness of substance or structure.

UK: Above average size, stalwart dog. Correctly proportioned, compact and

powerful form, permitting great strength, manoeuvrability and endurance.

These paragraphs are intended to give a quick first impression of the Rottweiler. While precise sizes are given in the next section, the picture is of a fairly large dog, bigger than a Boxer or Labrador and smaller than a Mastiff or Pyrenean. There is a clear demand for a powerful dog with strong bone combined with agility or manoeuvrability. It is made clear that sheer size, often combined with excess weight and flabbiness, is not desired. The use of the word 'compact', which the dictionary defines as "neatly fitted into a confined space" and "solid, firm", gives an excellent description of the Rottweiler.

The requirement in the AKC Standard that dogs should be larger, heavier-boned and more massive than bitches is important. This is a breed with marked differences between the sexes, and it should be obvious, even from a distance, whether you are looking at a dog or a bitch. We have always said that we like to be able to tell the sex of a Rottweiler when we are standing in front of it.

PROPORTIONS AND SIZE

ADRK: The length of the body measured from the point of the prosternum (breast bone) to the rear edge of the pelvic edge (ischial protuberance) should exceed the height at the highest point of the withers by 15 per cent.
Height of males 61 to 68 cm. Ideal size 65 to 66 cm.
Height of bitches 56 to 63 cm. Ideal size 60 to 61 cm.
Weight of males about 50 kilos.   Weight of bitches about 42 kilos.

AKC: Dogs 24 inches to 27 inches. Bitches 22 inches to 25 inches, with preferred size being mid-range of each sex. Correct proportion is of primary importance, as long as size is within the standard's range. The length of body from prosternum to the rearmost projection of the rump, is slightly longer than the height of the dog at the withers, the most desirable proportion of the height to length being 9 to 10. The Rottweiler is neither coarse nor shelly. Depth of chest is approximately fifty per cent of the height of the dog. His bone and muscle mass must be sufficient to balance his frame giving a compact and powerful appearance.

UK Dogs height at shoulder between 63 to 69 cm.(25-27 inches). Bitches between 58 to 63½ cm.(23-25 inches). Height should always be considered in relation to general appearance.

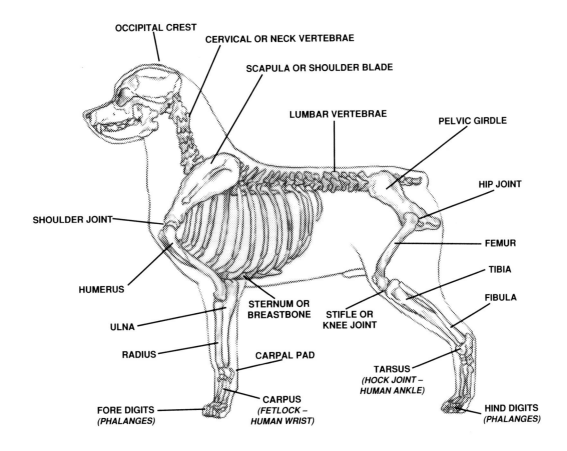

OCCIPITAL CREST

CERVICAL OR NECK VERTEBRAE

SCAPULA OR SHOULDER BLADE

LUMBAR VERTEBRAE

PELVIC GIRDLE

HIP JOINT

SHOULDER JOINT

FEMUR

TIBIA

HUMERUS

FIBULA

STERNUM OR
BREASTBONE

STIFLE OR
KNEE JOINT

ULNA

RADIUS

CARPAL PAD

TARSUS
*(HOCK JOINT –
HUMAN ANKLE)*

FORE DIGITS
(PHALANGES)

CARPUS
*(FETLOCK –
HUMAN WRIST)*

HIND DIGITS
(PHALANGES)

Anatomy of the Rottweiler

Note that the proportions of height to length and also chest depth are contained in the section on Body in both the UK and ADRK Standards .

We do not attach any importance to the apparent slight variations in size between the three Standards. The British Standard would appear to demand a slightly higher minimum size for both sexes, but the top height is almost the same for all three Standards. The variations that exist are probably the result of conversion between inches and centimetres, and the rounding-up of such figures, rather than a conscious desire to have height differences. The demand that the length should be slightly greater than the height at the withers should be noted. There is a tendency among some judges to select dogs, especially males, that are, in fact, square, because of their smart appearance. We also consider that a slightly greater length in proportion to height is acceptable in bitches. Failure to comply with the demand for a chest-

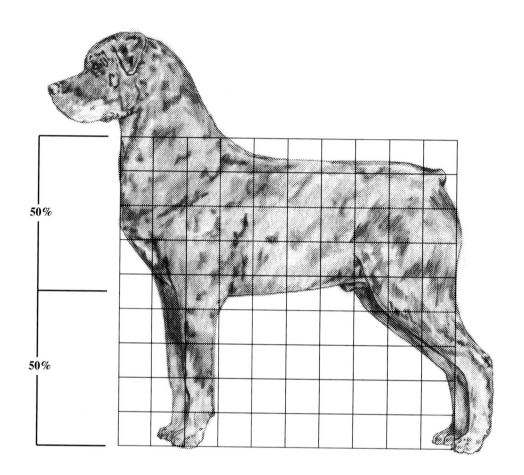

50%

50%

Size of the Rottweiler.

depth of 50 per cent of the height of the dog will result in an animal which is either short and squat on the leg, or one which is tall and leggy. The weights of 110lbs for dogs and 92½ lbs for bitches, given in the ADRK Standard are important. The Standards do not demand a massive dog, which inevitably loses manoeuvrability and is coarse and cloddy. Breeders who boast of dogs of 160lbs or more are losing sight of the original purpose of the breed.

CHARACTER AND TEMPERAMENT

ADRK: He is descended from friendly and peaceful stock and by nature loves

children, is affectionate, obedient, trainable and enjoys working. His rough appearance belies his ancestry. His demeanour is self-reliant, with strong nerves and fearless character. He is keenly alert to, and aware of, his surroundings.

AKC: The Rottweiler is basically a calm, confident and courageous dog with a self-assured aloofness that does not lend itself to immediate and indiscriminate friendships. A Rottweiler is self-confident and responds quietly and with a wait-and-see attitude to influences in his environment. He has an inherent desire to protect home and family, and is an intelligent dog of extreme hardness and adaptability with a strong willingness to work, making him especially suited as a companion, guardian and general all-purpose dog. The behaviour of the Rottweiler in the show ring should be controlled, willing and adaptable, trained to submit to examination of mouth, testicles, etc. An aloof or reserved dog should not be penalized, as this reflects the accepted character of the breed. An aggressive or belligerent attitude towards other dogs should not be faulted. A judge shall excuse from the ring any shy Rottweiler. A dog shall be judged fundamentally shy if, refusing to stand for examination, it shrinks away from the judge. A dog that in the opinion of the judge menaces or threatens him/her, or exhibits any sign that it may not be safely approached or examined by the judge in the normal manner, shall be excused from the ring. Any dog that in the opinion of the judge attacks any person in the ring shall be disqualified.

UK: Appearance displays boldness and courage. Self-assured and fearless. Calm gaze should indicate good humour. Good nature, not nervous, aggressive or vicious; courageous, biddable, with natural guarding instincts.

We have discussed the requirements of the Standards as to temperament and character in Chapter Two. In general, all Standards call for an intelligent, confident, courageous dog, easily trained, with natural guarding instincts. We find it surprising and indeed a little worrying that the AKC Standard contains no reference to any requirement for the Rottweiler to be good-humoured, good-natured, friendly and affectionate, as is asked for by the other two Standards.

The word 'affectionate' was in the AKC 1935 Standard, but it disappeared from the 1979 version. The demand for 'self-assured aloofness', which first appeared in the 1979 AKC Standard is not a requirement of either the ADRK or UK Standards. Apart from the comments that we made on this requirement in Chapter Two, we feel that there is a risk that such a requirement could lead to approval of a dog that was, in fact, hand-shy.

HEAD

Correct Head (front).   *Correct head (profile).*

ADRK: HEAD

SKULL Medium-long, the backskull broad between the ears, the forehead line seen from the side only moderately arched. The occiput is well developed without protruding excessively.

SKIN The skin on the head is tight-fitting but allowance is made for some wrinkling when dog is alert.

FOREFACE

NOSE The bridge of the muzzle is straight, broad at the base and slightly tapering. Nose is large, rather broad than round, always black with proportionately large nostrils.

MUZZLE Must never be long or short in comparison to the backskull.

LIPS Black close-lying with the corners closed, gums should be dark.

JAW Strong, broad upper and lower jaw.

CHEEKS Pronounced cheek bones (zygomatic arch).

DENTITION Complete (42 teeth), bite is strong with the upper incisors closing like scissors over those of the underjaw.

EYES Medium-large, almond-shaped, of dark brown colour with tightly fitting lids.

EARS Medium-large, pendant, triangular, set well apart and high. When brought forward, well placed ears will broaden the appearance of the backskull.

AKC: HEAD Of medium length, broad between the ears; forehead line seen in profile is moderately arched; zygomatic arch and stop well developed with strong broad upper and lower jaws. The desired ratio of backskull to muzzle is 3 to 2. Forehead is preferred dry, however, some wrinkling may occur when the dog is alert. EXPRESSION is noble, alert and self-assured.

Incorrect: 'wet'; excess loose neck skin.

EYES of medium size, almond-shaped with well fitting lids, moderately deep-set, neither protruding nor receding. The desired color is a uniform dark brown.

EARS of medium size, pendant, triangular in shape; when carried alertly the ears are level with the top of the skull and appear to broaden it. Ears are to be set well apart, hanging forward with the inner edge lying tightly against the head and terminating at approximately mid cheek.

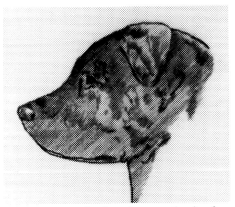

Incorrect: 'snipey'; note lack of muzzle depth and lack of stop.

MUZZLE Bridge is straight, broad at base with slight tapering towards tip. The end of the muzzle is broad with well developed chin. Nose is broad rather than round and always black.

LIPS Always black; corners closed; inner mouth pigment is preferred dark.

BITE AND DENTITION Teeth 42 in number (20 upper, 22 lower), strong, correctly placed, meeting in a scissors bite, lower incisors touching inside of upper incisors.

UK: HEAD AND SKULL Head medium length, skull broad between ears. Forehead moderately arched as seen from side.

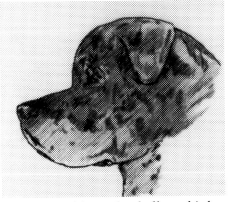

Incorrect: 'domey'; skull too high and rounded.

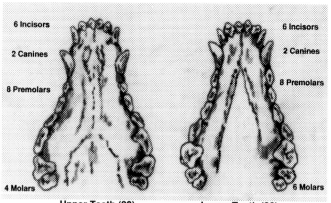

6 Incisors
2 Canines
8 Premolars
4 Molars

6 Incisors
2 Canines
8 Premolars
6 Molars

Upper Teeth (20) **Lower Teeth (20)**

Correct dentition.

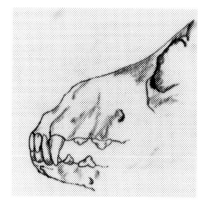

Correct: scissor bite.

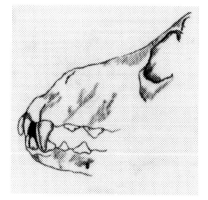

Incorrect: overshot.

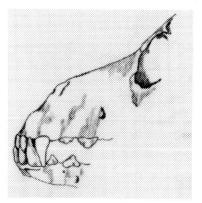

Incorrect: undershot.

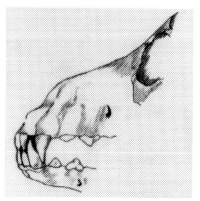

Incorrect: level/pincer bite.

Correct eyes.

Incorrect: Bird of prey (yellow) eyes

Incorrect: eyes of different size.

.Incorrect: eyes set too close.

Incorrect: eyes set too wide.

Incorrect: round eyes.

Incorrect: hairless lid.

Occipital bone well developed but not conspicuous. Cheeks well boned and muscled but not prominent. Skin on head not loose, although it may form a moderate wrinkle when attentive. Muzzle fairly deep with topline level and length of muzzle in relation to distance from well defined stop to occiput, to be as 2 is to 3. Nose is well developed with proportionately large nostrils, always black.

EYES Medium size, almond-shaped, dark brown in colour, light eye undesirable, eyelids close fitting.

EARS Pendant, small in proportion rather than large, set high and wide apart, lying flat and close to cheek.

MOUTH Teeth strong, complete dentition with scissor bite i.e. upper teeth closely overlapping the lower teeth and set square to the jaws. Flews black and firm, falling gradually away towards corners of mouth, which do not not protrude excessively.

While we would not like the Rottweiler to become a 'head breed', with the quality of the head becoming of overriding importance to the detriment of other features, there can be no doubt that the head of the Rottweiler is of major importance. A poor head on a dog can turn an otherwise attractive animal into a dull, uninteresting and untypical one. Head faults can vary from the over-large, round, coarse head, usually carrying too much wrinkle, to the long-muzzled, narrow, hound-like type. We like to think of a good Rottweiler head as forming a blunt-ended, inverted triangle when seen from above and in front. The top of the skull extended by the fold of the ears should form a virtually straight line, allowing only a slight rise of skull between the ears. Ear placement plays an important part in the quality of the head. When carried too high, and setting away from the skull, they give a terrier appearance, while low-set ears give a hound-like look to the head.

The term 'backskull', used in both the AKC and ADRK Standards, is not a term in common use in Britain. We suspect that its use in the ADRK Standard is the result of an American translation and not the term used in the original. While admitting that it is an accurate description of the rear part of the head, it is used in the AKC Standard to define the relative measurements of the skull and muzzle. We prefer the UK requirement which gives comparative measurements for the length of muzzle and the distance between stop and occiput. These datum points were used in the 1979 AKC Standard, and we feel that they gave a clearer definition. The problem is further confused for anyone reading the AKC and UK Standards by the fact that the two Standards reverse the measurements, although the final answer is the same.

Ears are an item on which the three Standards are beginning to diverge to a

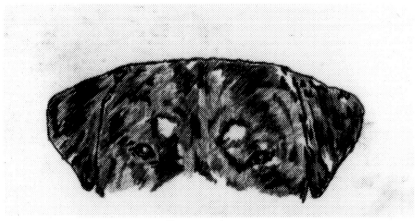

Correct ear set.

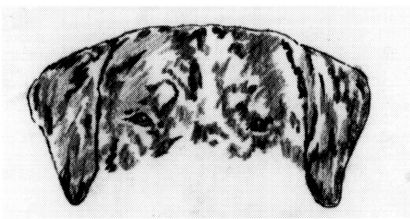

Incorrect: ears too large.

Incorrect: ears break at outer edge.

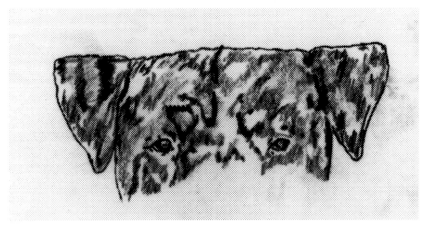

Incorrect: ears too high; 'terrier set'.

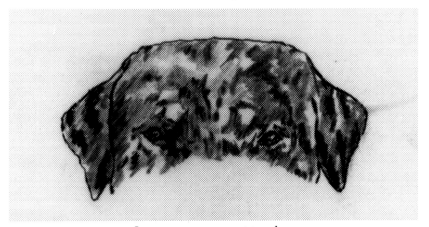

Incorrect: ears set too low.

Incorrect: 'rose' ear.

considerable extent. The 1970 ADRK standard asked for an ear that was "as small as possible". The 1979 AKC Standard stipulated "proportionately small", and the UK 1966 Standard stated "small in proportion, rather than large", and continues to demand the same in its current edition. However, the 1988 ADRK asks for ears that are "medium-large", while the AKC 1990 version states "medium size". We cannot see any good reason for this considerable change in the desirable size, and consider it to be a retrograde step. The relatively small, neat ear has always been an attractive feature of the Rottweiler head, and a large and inevitably pendulous ear has been considered a fault. Of course, it depends what you mean by large, medium and small. The change, which originated in Germany, was probably because some small ears tend to sit badly and to fly, but we personally feel that the "small in proportion" ear is still the type to aim for, provided that it is correctly placed and hangs close to the cheek.

The demand for an almond-shaped eye with close fitting lids is an example of the original purpose of the Rottweiler being reflected by the Standard. Such an eye was essential for a dog working cattle for long hours in a cloud of dust. The AKC requirement that the eye should be moderately deep-set needs consideration. The breed can suffer from entropion and it is all too easy to confuse this condition with the laid down requirements. Equally, the large round eye, apart from being incorrect, is extremely unattractive.

NECK

ADRK: Powerful, moderately long, well muscled, slightly arched, dry without dewlap or throatiness.

AKC: Powerful, well muscled, moderately long, slightly arched and without loose skin.

UK: Of fair length, strong, round and very muscular. Slightly arched, free from throatiness.

All three Standards seem to have difficulty in describing the desired length of neck. The correct length has to judged in conjunction with the overall size and balance of the dog, taking into account the thickness or diameter of the neck. A short 'bull neck' is often found with an upright shoulder. A 'ewe' neck, where the neck remains almost the same diameter for the whole of its length, is unattractive and such a neck can trap the inexperienced judge who may confuse it with elegance. A clean, well-

Correct (profile).

Incorrect: neck too long.

Incorrect: 'bull' neck.

Incorrect: 'ewe' neck.

arched neck can improve head carriage and add considerably to the overall quality of the dog. While it is undesirable, a very slight throatiness is almost unavoidable in a male, and is often exaggerated by the failure of the handler to place the collar correctly.

BODY

ADRK: BODY (TRUNK)
BACK Straight, strong, tight. Loin is short, strong and deep.
CROUP Broad, medium-long, gently sloping, neither flat nor steep.
CHEST Roomy, broad and deep (approximately 50 per cent of the height of the dog at the withers) with a well developed forechest and well arched ribs.
ABDOMEN Flanks not drawn up.
TAIL Docked short so that one or two tail vertebrae remain.

AKC: BODY
TOPLINE The back is firm and level extending in a straight line from behind the withers to the croup. The back remains horizontal to the ground while the dog is moving or standing.
BODY The chest is roomy, broad and deep, reaching to elbow, with well pronounced forechest and well sprung oval ribs. Back is straight and strong. Loin is short, deep and well muscled.
CROUP is broad, of medium length and only slightly sloping. Underline of a mature Rottweiler has a slight tuck-up. Males must have two normal testicles properly descended into the scrotum.
TAIL Tail docked short, close to body, leaving one or two tail vertebrae. The set

Correct body: illustrating correct topline, brisket, chest , ribs, loin croup and tail.
of the tail is more important than length. Properly set, it gives an impression of elongation of topline; carried slightly above horizontal when the dog is excited or moving.

UK: BODY Chest roomy, broad and deep with well sprung ribs. Depth of brisket will not be more, and not much less than 50 per cent of shoulder height. Back straight, strong and not too long, ratio of shoulder height to length of body should be as 9 is to 10, loins short, strong and deep, flanks not tucked up. CROUP of proportionate length, and broad, very slightly sloping.
TAIL normally carried horizontally, but slightly above horizontal when dog is alert. Customarily docked at the first joint, it is strong and not set too low.

Those of us who came into the breed some thirty or more years ago have tried very hard to maintain the original German concept of the breed. We therefore suffer a feeling almost of betrayal when some aspect of the dog is changed in the Standard. In the ADRK 1970 Standard the croup was required to be of medium length. The 1988 version now requires a croup which is medium-long. While the difference may be very little, many of us have admired a relatively short croup, and it would appear likely that the inclusion of the word 'long' will result in a lengthening of it. We also

Incorrect: soft topline or swayback.

Incorrect: high in rear, lacking rear angulation.

Incorrect: 'roach' back.

Brisket, Chest and Ribs.

Incorrect: short on leg.

Incorrect: too leggy.

Incorrect: long in body.

Incorrect: lack of forechest.

Loin, Croup and Tail.

Incorrect: sloping croup and low tail set.

Incorrect: tail held vertically.

find it surprising that the statement "underline of a mature Rottweiler has a slight tuck-up" has been inserted in the AKC 1990 Standard. The ADRK Standard has always required that the "flanks are not drawn up". A similar statement has always been in the UK Standard, and we would also question whether such a requirement is compatible with the demand for a deep loin contained in all three Standards. In the past, most of us have praised a dog who has a top and bottom line which are virtually parallel. If you look at the photograph of Int. and American Ch. Harras v Sofienbusch, featured in Chapter Ten, you will see an excellent example of this feature, and no one will deny that this dog has had worldwide acclaim. If you are being pedantic, and absolutely accurate, it is possible to say that a mature Rottweiler has a slight tuck-up, and such a tuck-up is more likely to be present in bitches than in dogs. However, items like this in Standards gradually become desirable, as opposed to acceptable, and we feel that this is an undesirable alteration. It is worth noting that the commentary to the 1986 ARC Illustrated Standard draws attention to the nearly level underline, and the fact that it is almost parallel to the topline. It goes on to state that a moderate tuck-up is evident on puppies, while a level underline appears on the adults. We are tempted to wonder whether the tuck-up, as stated in the AKC 1990 Standard, is a misprint and that it should in fact apply to "immature" Rottweilers.

FOREQUARTERS

ADRK: FOREQUARTERS
OVERALL Seen from the front, the forelegs are straight and not set close together. Seen from the side, the lower leg is straight. The shoulder angulation should approximate 45 degrees.
SHOULDER Well placed.
UPPER ARM Lying correctly on the body.
FOREARM Strongly developed and muscular.
PASTERN Somewhat springy, strong and not steep.
FEET Round, well closed and well knuckled, pads hard, nails short, black and strong.

AKC: FOREQUARTERS Shoulder blade is long and well laid back. Upper arm equal in length to shoulder blade, set so elbows are well under body. Distance from withers to elbow and elbow to ground is equal. Legs are strongly developed with straight, heavy bone, not set close together. Pasterns are strong, springy and almost perpendicular to the ground. Feet are round, compact with

Forequarters

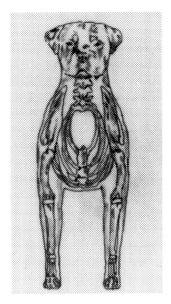

Correct front: legs and feet straight

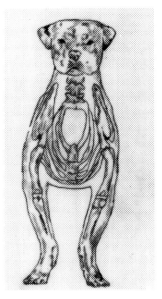

Incorrect: 'fiddle' front, pasterns bending in.

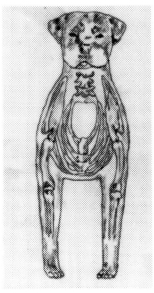

Incorrect: feet toe in.

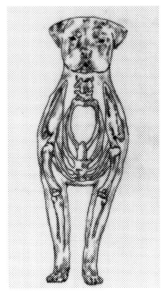

Incorrect: too narrow and toeing out.

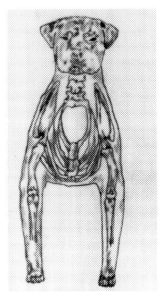

Incorrect: too wide.

Pasterns, Feet.

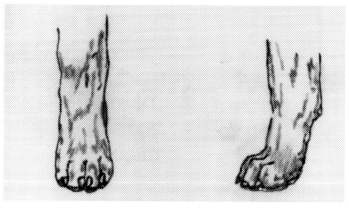

Correct foot.   Correct pastern and
foot profile.

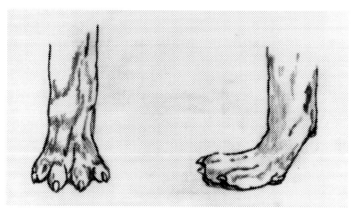

Incorrect: splayed foot.   Incorrect: 'soft' pastern
and 'flat' foot.

well arched toes, turning neither in nor out. Pads are thick and hard. Nails short, strong and black. Dewclaws may be removed.

UK: FOREQUARTERS Shoulders well laid back, long and sloping, elbows well let down but not loose. Legs straight, muscular, with plenty of bone and substance. Pasterns sloping slightly forward.

FEET Strong, round and compact with toes well arched. Pads very hard, toe nails short, dark and strong.

We prefer the AKC Standard for this section. Terms used in the ADRK Standard such as "well placed" and "lying correctly" are of little help, unless you already know the answer. However, the ADRK requirement that the shoulder angulation should be approximately 45 degrees, is worth noting. Perhaps this precise requirement can be best explained by saying that the shoulder blade should form a 45 degree angle, with a vertical line running through the shoulder joint. The slightly bent pastern is important for the welfare of the dog, as it acts as a shock absorber when jumping or moving. Front dew claws, which are normally left on in Europe, were in the past removed in Britain. However, some British breeders are now leaving on the front dew claws.

HINDQUARTERS

ADRK: HINDQUARTERS
OVERALL As seen from the rear, the rear legs are straight and not set close together. In a natural stance the articulation between the upper thigh and the lower thigh forms an obtuse angle.
UPPER THIGH Moderately long, broad and very muscular.
LOWER THIGH Long powerful and heavily muscled, sinewy with strong tendons, well angulated, not steep.
FEET Somewhat longer than the front feet, nevertheless tight knuckled, with strong toes, no dew claws.

AKC: HINDQUARTERS Angulation of hindquarters balances that of forequarters. Upper thigh is fairly long, very broad and well muscled. Stifle joint is well turned. Lower thigh is long, broad and powerful, with extensive muscling leading into a strong hock joint. Rear pasterns are nearly perpendicular to the ground. Viewed from the rear, hind legs are straight, strong and wide enough apart to fit with a properly built body.
FEET Are somewhat longer than the front feet, turning neither in nor out, equally compact with well arched toes. Pads are thick and hard. Nails short, strong and black. Dew claws must be removed.

UK: HINDQUARTERS. Upper thigh not too short, broad and strongly muscled. Lower thigh well muscled at top, strong and sinewy below. Stifles

Hindquarters

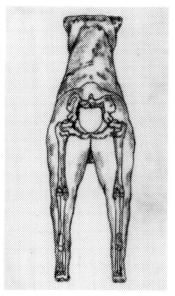

Correct rear: legs and feet straight

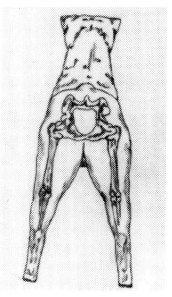

Incorrect: too wide.

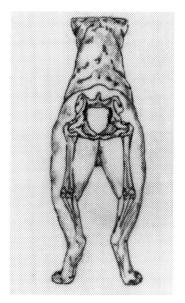

Incorrect: hocking in and/or toeing out.

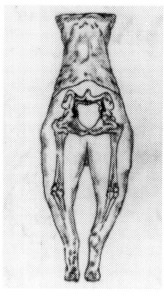

Incorrect: too narrow at hocks.

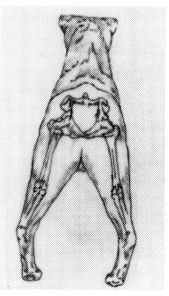

Incorrect: hocking out and/or toeing in.

Stifle joint, lower thigh.

Incorrect; under-angulated and too short in hock.

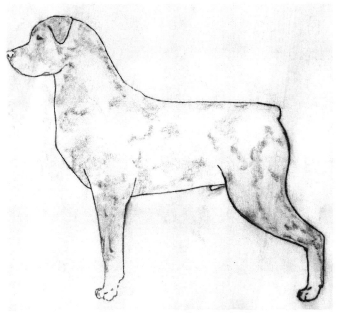

Incorrect: too much angulation.

fairly well bent. Hocks well angulated without exaggeration, metatarsals not completely vertical. Strength and soundness of hock highly desirable.
FEET Strong, round and compact with toes well arched. Hind feet somewhat longer than front. Pads very hard, toenails short, dark and strong. Rear dew claws removed.

We find the ADRK description of the articulation between the upper and lower thigh confusing, and attempts to clarify it by reference to the 1970 and 1981 ADRK Standards only made matters worse. We prefer the AKC statement that "angulation of hindquarters balances that of forequarters". If you substitute "reflects" for "balance" and look at the skeletal structure of the Rottweiler, you will see that the femur lies roughly parallel to the scapula or shoulder blade, while the tibia lies in the same plane as the humerus. Out of all the rather obscure statements in the three Standards, we arrive at the fact that a Rottweiler should be neither under nor over angulated. It is best summed up by the statement that it should not be as straight in stifle as a Mastiff nor as angulated as a German Shepherd Dog. We see no reason for the use of the word 'metatarsals' in the UK Standard. and we prefer the easily understood term 'rear pastern', as used by the AKC. We would comment on the question of rear dew claws. The AKC and UK ask that rear dew claws should be removed. The ADRK merely states "no dew claws". It is not unusual to find quite large, or even double dew claws on a Rottweiler. We have formed the opinion that a dog that has had the hind dew claw removed tends to be cow hocked. We do not know whether it is caused by the removal of the dew claw – bearing in mind that, if present, it is the first metatarsal bone – or if dogs that have a hind dew claw are likely to be cow hocked in any case. Either way, it is quite easy to reduce the incidence of hind dew claws by selective breeding, and for many years we have not bred from stock that carries them.

MOVEMENT

ADRK: M0VEMENT The Rottweiler is a trotter. The back remains firm and relatively motionless. The gait is harmonious, positive, powerful and free, with long strides.

AKC: GAIT The Rottweiler is a trotter. His movement should be balanced, harmonious, sure, powerful and unhindered, with strong forereach and a powerful rear drive. The motion is effortless, efficient and ground covering. Front and rear legs are thrown neither in nor out, as the imprint of hind feet

Gait

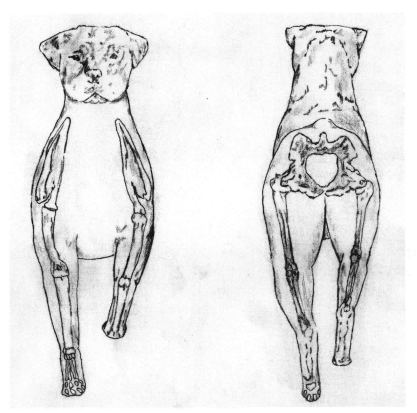

Correct: coming.   *Correct: going*

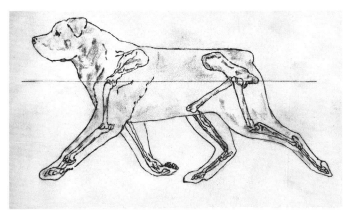

Correct gait: trot.

Incorrect gait: pace.

should touch that of forefeet. In a trot the forequarters and hindquarters are mutually coordinated, while the back remains level, firm and relatively motionless. As speed increases the legs will converge under body towards a centre line.

UK: GAIT/MOVEMENT Conveys an impression of supple strength, endurance and purpose. While back remains firm and stable there is a powerful hindthrust and good stride. First and foremost, movement should be harmonious, positive and unrestricted.

We have never been very happy with the use of the word "supple" in the UK Standard. It is acceptable if interpreted as easy and graceful, but it must not be considered to mean pliant, elegant or willowy. Many judges expect that a dog moving toward them should, ideally, keep its front legs straight and parallel. We are therefore glad that the AKC Standard points out that this is mechanically incorrect, and that the legs will converge towards the centre line as speed increases. The powerful drive by the hindquarters is a vital aspect of the Rottweiler's movement, and its absence should be condemned by judges. It is important to remember that one of the Rottweiler's functions was to herd cattle, a duty which demanded long hours at a steady trot – hence the emphasis on the breed being a "trotter" in both the ADRK and AKC Standards. In the show ring, judges must accept that this is the correct speed of movement. Occasionally judges will demand that the dog be moved at a walk, on the grounds that this will reveal movement faults – it certainly will, as this is not the speed that the dog is designed for; a slow-walking Rottweiler is an uncoordinated amble. A fault sometimes seen in fore and aft movement is crabbing.

While it is true that a few Rottweilers do move in this fashion, the fault is often created in the show ring by the handler either keeping the lead too short, or by the dog pulling to the side as a result of some other attraction.

COAT

ADRK: COAT QUALITY Consisting of outer coat and under coat. The outer coat is medium long, coarse, thick and straight. The under coat must not show through the outer coat. On the back of the rear legs the hair is somewhat longer.

AKC: COAT Outer coat is straight, coarse, dense, of medium length and lying flat. Undercoat should be present on neck and thighs, but the amount is influenced by climatic conditions. Undercoat should not show through outer coat. The coat is shortest on head, ears and legs, longest on breeching. The Rottweiler is to be exhibited in the natural condition with no trimming.

UK: COAT Consists of top coat and undercoat. Top coat is of medium length, coarse and flat. Undercoat, essential on the neck and thighs, should not show through top coat. Hair may also be a little longer on the back of the forelegs and breechings. Long or excessively wavy coat highly undesirable.

Although it has always been accepted that the undercoat is only required on the neck and thighs, it is, in fact, frequently found on the rest of the body. The ADRK Standard accepts this and does not attempt to specify the precise positions. Although all three Standards state that the undercoat should not show through the top coat, this is, to a certain extent, dependent on whether the dog is moulting, and in our opinion, judges should make allowances for this. Wide variations of climate in the U.S.A. have caused the AKC to point out that the undercoat may be affected by climatic conditions. We have memories of a lady from California, who announced that all British Rottweilers were long-coated. We had to point out that the Rottweiler, being a sensible dog, had shed much of its cold weather coat in the warmth of California.

COLOUR

ADRK: COLOUR Black with sharply defined dark reddish-brown markings on the cheeks, muzzle, under the neck, on the chest and legs and also over the eyes and under the tail.

AKC: COLOR: Always black with rust to mahogany markings. The demarcation between black and rust is to be clearly defined. The markings should be located as follows: a spot over each eye; on cheeks; as a strip around each side of muzzle, but not on the bridge of the nose; on throat; triangular mark on both sides of prosternum; on forelegs from carpus downwards to the toes; on inside of rear legs showing down the front of the stifle and broadening out to front of rear legs from hock to toes, but not completely eliminating black from rear of pasterns; under tail; black pencilling on toes. The undercoat is gray, tan or black. Quantity and location of rust markings is important and should not exceed ten per cent of body colour.

UK: COLOUR Black with clearly defined markings as follows: a spot over each eye, on cheeks, as a strip around each side of muzzle, but not on bridge of nose, on throat, two clear triangles on either side of the breast bone, on forelegs from carpus downward to toes, on inside of rear legs from hock to toes, but not completely eliminating black from back of legs, under tail. Colour of markings from rich tan to mahogany and should not exceed 10 per cent of body colour. White marking is highly undesirable. Black pencil markings on toes are desirable. Undercoat is grey, fawn, or black.

If you want an accurate, and easy-to-understand description of the colour requirements for the Rottweiler, use the AKC version. The UK Standard contains a 'nonsense' in its description of the colour on the back legs when it states that the tan markings should be only from hock to toes. Due to a quirk of genetics, the markings on a black-and-tan dog are virtually identical, with only slight variations of degree, but not of positioning, whether the dog is a Rottweiler, a Gordon Setter, a Dachshund, a mongrel or any other black-and-tan breed. For this reason, little attempt was made to give a precise location for the markings. It was assumed that everybody knew. The ADRK standard tends to retain this viewpoint, and we have considerable sympathy with it. We find the ten per cent limit on markings in the AKC and UK Standards a little absurd, and we do not believe that a judge can be expected to make this sort of calculation in the ring. Your eye and experience should be able to tell you if the markings are too little or excessive. We do not intend to argue over the relative merits of "rust" and "rich tan" as a description of the markings. There is general agreement that the dark brown or mahogany is the desirable colour, with a slightly lighter colour being acceptable. The very light straw colour is very unattractive, and often accompanies an excessive amount of markings.

FAULTS

ADRK: FAULTS
OVERALL Light boned, poorly muscled, insufficient leggy appearance.
HEAD Houndy, too narrow, weak, too short, too long or too coarse, shallow forehead (faulty or insufficient stop).
FOREFACE Long or pointed muzzle, ram's or split nose, convex or concave bridge of the muzzle, light or spotted nose.
LIPS Open pink coloured or flecked lips, or lips with open corners.
JAW Narrow underjaw.
CHEEKS Over-prominent cheeks.
BITE Level bite.
EARS Too low set, heavy, long, leather too thin, pulled back in such a manner as to stick up, and ears that are not properly carried.
EYES Light in colour, protruding i.e. lids not fitting tightly, too deep set, too big or too round eyes.
NECK Too long, thin, poorly muscled neck, dewlap or throaty.
BODY Too long, too short, narrow.
CHEST Flat-ribbed rib cage, round rib cage, shallow rib cage.
BACK Too long, weak or sway backed, roach backed.
CROUP Steep croup, too short, too flat or too long.
TAIL Too high set or too low set.
FOREQUARTERS Narrow set or crooked forelegs. Straight shoulder, faulty or deficient elbow placement, too long, too short or too straight upper arm; weak or straight pasterns; spread toes, too flat or too arched toes, stunted toes, light nails.
HINDQUARTERS Poorly muscled thighs, sickle-hocked or cow-hocked or bow legged, too little or too much angulation. Dew claws.
SKIN Wrinkled skin on head.
COAT CONDITION Soft, too short, too long coat, curly coat, lacking undercoat.
COLOUR Incorrect colour, poorly defined, too extensive markings.

AKC: FAULTS
SIZE AND PROPORTION Lack of proportion, undersized, oversized, reversal of sex characteristics (bitchy dogs, doggy bitches).
EYES Yellow (bird of prey) eyes, eyes of different color or size, hairless eye rim.
EARS Improper carriage (creased, folded or held away from cheek/head.

MUZZLE Total lack of mouth pigment (pink mouth).
BITE AND DENTITION Level bite; any missing tooth.
COAT Wavy coat. Open, excessively short, or curly coat; total lack of undercoat; any trimming that alters the length of the natural coat.
COLOR Straw-colored, excessive, insufficient or sooty markings; rust marking, other than described above; white marking any place on dog (a few rust or white hairs do not constitute a marking).
SUMMARY The foregoing is a description of the ideal Rottweiler. Any structural fault that detracts from the above described working dog must be penalized to the extent of the deviation.

DISQUALIFYING FAULTS

ADRK: OVERALL Obvious reversal of sex characteristics (bitchy dogs and the reverse).
DEMEANOUR Anxious, shy, cowardly, gun-shy, vicious, excessively suspicious (distrustful), nervous.
EYES Entropion, ectropion, yellow eyes, two eyes of different colour.
DENTITION Overshot, undershot, dogs with missing pre-molars or molars.
TESTICLES Unilateral cryptorchid or cryptorchid males. Both testicles must be well developed and properly descended into the scrotum.
COAT Exceptionally long and curly coated dogs.
COLOUR Dogs that do not have the typical black ground colour in combination with correctly placed brown markings; white marks.

AKC: EYES Entropion. Ectropion.
BITE AND DENTITION Overshot, undershot, (when incisors do not touch or mesh); wry mouth, two or more missing teeth.
BODY Unilateral cryptorchid or cryptorchid males.
COAT Long coat.
COLOR Any base color other than black; absence of all markings.
TEMPERAMENT A dog that, in the opinion of the judge, attacks any person in the ring.

The ADRK and the AKC include 'disqualifying faults', and a judge is required to dismiss any dog from the ring which he considers to have such a fault, irrespective of any virtues it may possess. The British Kennel Club does not accept disqualifying faults, and argues that a judge should consider all faults against virtues and make a decision based on his assessment of the overall dog. While we agree with this in principle, we believe that it is desirable to introduce disqualifying faults with regard to temperament. With regard to other faults, the British Standard does not, in general, include faults, except for a blanket statement that: "Any departure from the foregoing points should be considered a fault and the seriousness with which the fault should be regarded should be in exact proportion to its degree."

We consider that the listing of faults in a Standard is of value as an added explanation and amplification of what is, and what is not desirable, and that they are a useful aid to any person studying the breed. While a judge working to the British Standard cannot disqualify a dog for a fault, we would be surprised if such a judge gave a high placing to a dog which had a fault listed in the other two Standards as meriting disqualification. All judges are obviously required to judge to the Standard of the country in which they are judging. However, we consider that a study of all three Standards can be of great assistance in understanding the Rottweiler, with each Standard complementing and amplifying the others.

All three Standards, at present, require the Rottweiler to have a docked tail. In Europe, and possibly elsewhere in the world, there is a likelihood that this requirement will change in the near future. As with other docked breeds, Rottweiler owners have always known their breed with its short docked tail. They know that the docking operation is so simple and painless that there has never been a need to worry about the actual act of docking, or the effect it might have on the dog's adult life. Many generations of breeding have created a dog whose conformation and balanced appearance requires the short tail; its total appearance and construction would be changed by the addition of a long tail. This was as it had always been, and the idea of change did not enter people's heads.

However, in the mid Eighties agitation started amongst the veterinary profession that docking was cruel, and it was described as an "unnecessary mutilation". The vets totally ignored the wide range of mutilations that they, and the farmers, carried out on farm animals. These 'mutilations', many of them far more painful and serious than the removal of a puppy's tail, were condoned on the ground that they were economically expedient. In other words, cruelty is acceptable provided it is profitable. The result of this agitation was the formation of a European committee consisting almost entirely of veterinary surgeons, acting under the Council of Europe and the Treaty of Rome. This committee eventually produced a convention on the welfare of pet animals, and included in the convention was a requirement that docking should be banned. Under the Treaty of Rome, such conventions do not become law, but the signatory countries are morally bound to introduce legislation implementing the recommendations. As soon as these proposals became known, there were protests from dog organisations all over Europe, with varying degrees of success. A number of countries have lost the battle, so that it is now illegal to dock a dog for non-therapeutic reasons. Germany has so far succeeded in resisting such legislation, while Britain has arrived at what is known as the compromise solution, whereby docking for cosmetic reasons is legal only if carried out by a veterinary surgeon. This, of course, depends on the goodwill of the vets, and there are signs that their governing body may try to declare that it is unethical for their members to carry out the operation. If they do this, it will, of course, be a betrayal of the spirit in which the agreement was made.

There are already a number of countries who cannot comply with the requirements of the F.C.I. Standard with regard to docking, and this number may increase. The situation raises a number of problems such as the situation when someone wants to import a dog from a country where docking is banned to a country, such as America, where it is a requirement of the Standard. Do you dock the dog, as an adult, on its arrival in the States? The docking of an adult is, of course, a far more serious and painful operation than the docking of a puppy, and there is the question of whether the docking of a mature adult will affect its balance and movement. Alternatively, is America going to deny itself the opportunity to import stock from Europe? It was repeatedly pointed out during the dispute that the measure was likely to create far more pain and cruelty than was ever caused by docking.

If the breed is to be faced with Rottweilers with long tails, the next question has to be 'What sort of a tail do we want?' One of the opponents of docking has said: "You will just have to breed for the correct tail." No-one, of course, can tell us what is a correct tail. Do we want a tail that is carried high over the back (often called a sickle tail)? Do we want it down to the hocks, in the style of a German Shepherd Dog? We believe that if we wish to retain the present sturdy hindquarters and desirable croup, then we shall have to settle for a tail carried high, and possibly over the back – at least when the dog is alert. Any attempt to breed for a tail hanging down to the hocks will result in a change in both the croup and hindquarters. The answer may lie in the item in the present Standards which requires the tail to be an elongation of the topline. This is like the tail of the Labrador, which is similar in thickness and length, and, as stipulated in the Breed Standard, "it may be carried gaily but should not curl over the back." One further item of cruelty that will be created by any ban on docking is that some Rottweilers are born with kinked or twisted tails. Whatever the type of tail which we decide on, no one will want these defects, and if tail docking is banned, puppies carrying these 'faults' will almost certainly be put down.

Illustrations produced with permission from the American Rottweiler Club Illustrated Standard. Illustrations by Pamela Anderson, all rights reserved, Anderson Studios Inc.

An undocked Rottweiler with the tail carried up and over.

An undocked Rottweiler with tail carried down to the hocks.

Chapter Nine

THE SHOW RING

If you set out to breed Rottweilers with the intention of producing stock which is physically good-looking in accordance with the Breed Standard, there is only one place that you can prove to yourself and the rest of the world that you have achieved your object, and that is in the show ring. You could, of course, have a collection of magnificent animals sitting in your kennels – magnificent in your opinion – but unless you submit them to the critical eyes of the show ring, their magnificence will continue to be in your eyes only, and you will probably be wrong. The show ring is where you prove or fail to prove the quality of your stock. In our opinion, there is a vast difference between taking a dog to a show with the aim of allowing a judge and the ringside to assess its quality, hoping it will be good enough to win, and taking a dog to a show with the sole aim of winning, irrespective of its quality. We hope that you breed, and show, with the aim of improving the breed, rather than merely wanting to win in the show ring. Unfortunately, there are many exhibitors who appear to be indifferent to the quality of the stock that they show, provided that they can persuade the judge to give the dog the desired award card. Obviously, this approach requires the co-operation of the judge, an aspect which we will discuss later in this chapter.

There are, of course, many people who breed numerous litters of pedigree dogs, who never go near the show ring. Few of the puppies that they produce are sold to exhibitors, for the obvious reason that exhibitors prefer to buy from stock that has proved its quality in the ring. The bulk of the puppies sold by this type of breeder go into pet homes, purchased by people who neither know, nor care, about the finer points of the breed. Such breeders may produce excellent pets, but as the aim of the exercise is to make money, it is doubtful whether physical quality has a very high priority.

Showing dogs can be very rewarding. There is enormous satisfaction in winning a top award with a dog that is the result of several generations of selective breeding, stretching over several years. It is the product of disappointments and triumphs, careful rearing and training. If you believe that you can go out and buy a puppy, and start showing in the certainty that you will immediately achieve top honours, then you will almost certainly be disappointed. Success in the show ring requires hard work, patience and dedication. Furthermore, if you do succeed in winning, and even if your first dog becomes a Champion, it does not mean that you are an expert. It merely means that you are lucky.

If you decide on a career in the show ring you will probably decide that you would like a kennel-name, which is usually known as a prefix, although technically, it may be a prefix or a suffix. In our opinion, kennel clubs should not issue prefixes, unless a kennel has established by breeding and showing that it capable of producing high-quality stock. In other words, a prefix should be an indication of quality, and not just a trade name. Kennel club prefixes carry considerable status in the eyes of the general public, and are used as a selling point by many kennels. The public is often unaware that a prefix can be obtained simply by paying a fee, and is unable to differentiate between a famous name with years of knowledge and success behind it, and the prefix that was bought yesterday by a complete beginner. Modern attitudes mean that everyone demands instant success and status, and can see no reason why, if a breeder with forty years of experience behind them has a prefix, the newcomer should not have the same. Regrettably, Kennel Clubs seem to bow to this sort of pressure. If you do decide that you wish to have a prefix, then there are a number of factors to consider. There are many thousands of prefixes, and your first problem will be to find one that is attractive to you, but that has not been used already by somebody else. Do not try and achieve reflected glory by using a famous prefix belonging to someone else, even if you can legally get away with it – for example if the prefix is registered overseas, and therefore is not protected in your country: you

Larry and Judy Elsden judging at Richmond, 1990.

may fool other beginners, but you will only attract the contempt of the knowledgeable. The same thing applies if you take a well-known prefix and change one letter. The Kennel Club computer will accept that it is a different word, but everyone else will see through your deception. Many of us have to spend time and money trying to prevent the theft of our prefixes, which are coveted by people who do not wish to earn them in the hard way that we did. Also, if you are wise, you will make a choice that cannot be mispronounced. Our own prefix 'Chesara' was taken from the song Che Sara Sara, pronounced Kay Sir Ra, and meaning "whatever will be, will be". It seemed an appropriate choice at the beginning of a long and uncertain show career. However, it has been pronounced by the uninitiated in a wide variety of ways, varying from something that sounds like a laxative to the 'cheesy ear Rottweilers'. We once had a telephone call at two o'clock on the morning from some very drunken dog people we had never heard of. They were having a party and an argument had started: would we settle a bet and tell them the correct pronunciation of our prefix? We told them, and suggested that they sent us half the value of the bet – and went back to bed musing on some of the disadvantages of having a famous prefix.

There are three ways in which you can enter the show ring: as an exhibitor, as a steward, or as a judge. We do not intend to cover the duties of stewards, other than to suggest that working as a steward can be useful experience for the aspiring judge. It enables you to watch and listen to a judge at work, and to a certain extent, you can see the dogs as he sees them. However, long before you take a judging appointment, we hope that you will be an exhibitor. Surprisingly, there are a few judges who avoid this stage – not, we might add, without detriment to their judging ability. We propose to start, as you should, with exhibiting – which means handling. In an ideal world, it would be the quality of the dog, and only the dog, that decided its final placing in a class. In fact, success is achieved by a combination of dog and handler. This certainly applies in Britain and the U.S.A., and to a slightly lesser extent in Germany, where examination is much more detailed and takes very much longer. Even there, handling and training play a significant part. The art of handling can be described as the ability to show your dog to its best advantage, while at the same time concealing its faults from the judge. Conversely, part of the skill in judging is the ability to spot the faults of the dog, in spite of the handler's attempts to conceal them. You may feel that we are suggesting that a clever handler can win with a poor dog. This is not really true, although it can depend on the ability of the judge. However, good handling can improve a poor dog, and it is even more true to say that a poor handler can ruin the chances of a good dog.

It is possible to identify three basic methods of handling: the German, the American – often described as 'stacking' – and the British free-standing method, usually involving baiting. To a considerable extent, the three methods overlap, with all countries using aspects of each method. It is largely true to say that a good handler is born not made. Some people have a natural ability to get the best out of their dogs, while others have to work hard to learn the skills required. The very best handlers have the natural ability, but also take time and trouble to perfect their methods. To illustrate the art of handling, we have enlisted the help of a handler who, in our opinion, is the best Rottweiler handler in the British show ring today. Like the rest of us, Liz Dunhill learnt the hard way. We will let her describe her first attempts at handling.

"Most people buy their first Rottweiler as a pet, and some eventually go to a dog show and get the showing bug. Frequently, a newcomer comes to me and says: 'I wish I could handle like you, you make it look so easy'. Well, I started out in the same way as most other people, with my pet Rott named Max. Sired by a Champion, and with lots of other Champions in his pedigree, I felt that the judge would be awestruck by such a magnificent specimen. The only thing I did not think of was that it was not his pedigree on the other end of the lead – it was my large, gawky, long-nosed, long-backed, bitchy-looking male. He had curtains of skin hanging from his neck and around his face, and resembled a Shar Pei more than a Rott. There I was, with my thick choke-chain, a six-foot-long training lead, and no bait. I walked into the ring and stood there as if I was waiting for a bus. The steward shouted "Stand your dogs!" This was when the trouble started. I picked up Max at the front, and he firmly plonked his rear on the floor. I then lifted him up by the middle, and held him rigidly. At this stage, he looked like a cross between a donkey and a camel, and my six-foot-long lead was neatly tangled around my dog's front feet. The judge approached. Max looked at him with a worried look, obviously thinking that Mum had gone mad, and sat down again. I pulled at one end and pushed at the other, and finished up with the lead around everybody's legs. We spent five minutes trying to look at his teeth, and then made an equally disastrous attempt at showing his movement. I achieved fourth place in a class of four, and left the ring with instructions from a purple-faced judge, telling me "to go and learn how to handle". Once I had recovered from my first reaction, which was never to go near a dog show again, I decided to take the judge's advice and do just that – learn how to handle."

Liz Dunhill watched the top Rottweiler handlers, asked advice, and practised with her dog in front of a mirror. Eventually she won a first prize with Max – an event which taught her that a good handler can make a poor dog look better. However, not satisfied with what she could learn in Britain, she went to Germany and watched the handlers there, and then to the U.S.A. In America she not only watched, she also got the opportunity to handle both Rottweilers and Akitas in the show ring. She developed a thorough knowledge of both the British and American methods, and it is probably true to say that her own style in the ring combines the best of both. Talking with Liz, you cannot help but be impressed at the amount of thought and effort that goes into her handling – an excellent example of what is needed in order to succeed.

In Germany the dog is encouraged to show itself off by attraction by a second person, or by letting it spar up to another dog. The latter method works particularly well with a male by encouraging its natural aggression. It results in a very noisy ring, with dogs snarling at each other. It also requires a large ring with plenty of space to prevent the dogs actually reaching each other, and it would not be accepted by the British Kennel Club, as Liz Dunhill remarks, you do not need to handle – just hang on tight to your end of the lead! In any case, attraction by a second person, known as double handling, is not allowed under British rules. We, personally, have no real objection to double handling, provided that it does not interfere with other dogs or handlers. We do not believe that you can really legislate against the husband at the ringside who suddenly develops a bad cough when his wife is showing their dog. Although it broke a long list of rules, we once saw a wonderful example of

The dog is encouraged to show itself off by attraction by a second person, or by letting it spar up to another dog. *Russell Fine Art.*

Stacking entails the handler placing the dog manually into the correct position. *Russell Fine Art.*

double handling at a show in Germany. The handler ordered his dog to stand, threw the lead on the floor, walked to the opposite corner of the ring and attracted his dog from there. The dog stood perfectly, and looked magnificent. The judge was able to move around him, and look at him from all angles. Apart from being illegal under British rules, it takes a lot of training to show a dog like this.

Stacking in the American style involves using the type of collar described in Chapter Four as an American collar or control collar. The collar is placed tightly under the jaw and held behind the ears in a way that shows off the crest of neck, ear-set and shape of the jaw-line. Each leg is placed into position manually by the handler, who controls the dog and keeps the head still by holding the collar in the other hand. The dog's expression and outline is enhanced by baiting with a piece of liver or some other titbit. Although Liz has used a white collar in the photograph, so that you can see its positioning, she would normally use a black one.

Ch. Fantasa Simply Red, being taught to show American-style.

Stage 1: Walk the dog into position with the collar in your left hand, short lead dropped down the right side of the dog, out of sight, and guide the dog's head and push into position with your right hand.

Russell Fine Art.

*Stage 2: Holding collar in
left hand, transfer dog's
body weight on to left
foreleg. Pick up the right
leg by the elbow, move the
elbow away from the body
and set the leg down under
the shoulder.*

Russell Fine Art.

*Stage 3: Repeat stage 2
with the left leg, by holding
the collar in the right hand,
pulling the dog's weight on
to the right leg. Pick up the
elbow, and set down to
match the other leg. On
this photo, you can see the
elbow pulled away from the
body, and the short lead on
the dog's off-side.*

Russell Fine Art.

Stage 4: Hold the collar in the right hand, keeping the dog's head in position, and steady the dog with the left hand. Do not allow the dog to lean against your legs.

Russell Fine Art.

Stage 5: Move the rear left leg by grasping the leg by the hock, and work the joint with fingers and thumb, setting the rear pastern down straight.

Russell Fine Art.

Stage 6: Repeat the same procedure with the right hock.

Russell Fine Art.

Stage 7: Switch the collar to the left hand, and use bait to achieve expression. This picture shows the positioning of the collar in the fingers, which are locked into position giving space to show off the crest of the neck. Shortening the collar and locking it between the fingers also stops the dog from backing out of his collar.

Russell Fine Art.

Ch. Fantasa Simply Red has not been previously trained in the American style, but this shows that it can be done.

Russell Fine Art.

Liz now shows handling in the free-standing English style, and we must make a small claim for fame here. Having come into Rottweilers from Boxers, which were usually shown stacked in the American fashion, with the handler kneeling in what was known as the prayer-mat position, topping and tailing the dog, we decided that this would not do for Rottweilers. We developed the free-standing position using cooked liver as bait, and as liver is messy stuff to put in your pocket – we made a small bait-bag with tapes to tie around the waist. Seeing their popularity today, we wish that we had patented the idea. It would have made us a fortune!

Since nearly all exhibitors in the U.K. are owner-handlers, their dogs are usually companions as well as show dogs. Free standing is achieved by having a rapport with your dog and working as a team. The dog is taught to stand in front of the handler, its eyes focusing on the bait-pouch, worn around the waist. The dog is conditioned from a baby that 'stand' means food, and it is trained to stare fixedly at a hand in a pocket, because there is usually a biscuit in there somewhere. If Liz is in the kitchen and puts her hand into her dog-walking coat, every Rott stands in front of her, in a show pose, jostling for pole position, with eyes glued on her pocket and then up at her face, and they are all saying: 'Go on, give us a biscuit.' "Most of my training is done in the kitchen - no lead and totally informal," says Liz. People automatically assume that I spend hours training my dogs when, in fact, it is done in any odd spare moment. The pups are also taught to follow me around the lawn from the age of eight weeks. They just follow the food and my voice, without a lead, so that by the time the lead training starts they have already bonded to me and will follow me everywhere, having learnt to respond to my voice and body language.

Puppies should start show-training at an early age, and Liz shows how to teach an eight-week-old puppy to accept being 'gone over' and having its legs placed.

BRITISH STYLE

Fantasa Crimson Cavalier showing that free-standing can be achieved without a collar and lead. This method is the most widely used in the UK,although not as shown here, without a lead.   Hartley

Puppy Training

Stage 1: Walk the pup into position with food in the hand and place the rear, keeping it distracted with the bait. Allow it to lick at the food, but keep it cupped tightly in your hand.

Russell Fine Art.

Stage 2: Set up the front leg first.

Russell Fine Art.

Stage 3: Then set the front right leg. If the puppy sits down, keep lifting her up by the tummy and steady her. Use the command "stand" at the same time.
Russell Fine Art.

This shows the baby Clockwork Orange topped and tailed.
Russell Fine Art.

Training the youngster

Stage 1: Hold the bait and lead up high, so that the dog cranes his neck skywards. Then lean your upper body over the dog's head; this will put him off balance and he will have to walk backwards, which sets his back feet parallel.

Russell Fine Art.

Stage 2: If a leg has to be moved, the principles are the same as for stacking, except that the dog is kept distracted with liver. This will keep him happy. Always feed the dog with the right hand and move the legs with the left, so that he does not become confused. He will expect to be fed with the one hand only.

Stage 3: The right hand continues to bait the dog, while the the left hand leans across the shoulder, picks up the elbow, moves the dog's front forward and places the left leg in position. The same procedure is used for the right leg.
                    Russell Fine Art.

Stage 3a: The same effect as stage 3 can be achieved by baiting the dog forward, and walking him into position.
Russell Fine Art.

This photograph shows the dog set up, and the handler standing to one side to allow the judge to view its front.
Russell Fine Art.

King Crimson watching for a piece of liver. Note that the handler is standing back from the dog. Once the training is more advanced, you will be able to increase the distance between dog and handler, and you will be able to lower your hands a little more to bring his head further down.

Russell Fine Art.

She also uses this method to assess each puppy in a litter so as to gain an idea of its overall shape and conformation. It also helps to prepare the puppy for life in its new home. Liz goes on to show Fantasa King Crimson being schooled in the basic techniques. He is still a puppy and lacks concentration, but he is keen and loves his food. She was once given a useful tip by an experienced Rottweiler handler, who suggested that a dog should be taught to walk backwards and to avoid getting trapped in the corner of the ring. Liz took this a step further, and now uses this method to set up the dog's rear end. With a schooled dog, all you need to do is move your upper body slightly forward and say "Back". The dog will understand your body language and respond.

Liz goes on to describe the training needed so that a dog will allow its teeth to be examined.

"I would say that one of the main problems while judging is having to struggle to see a dog's teeth. A dog should be trained to having its bite and mouth examined, from the time that it is a young puppy. The pup should be held by an assistant, and the trainer firmly grasps the puppy by the skin around the face, saying "Teeth", and then gently lifts up the lips, followed by lots of praise. If the puppy complains and struggles, give it a firm shake, say "No", and try again. Do not constantly keep looking at the puppy's teeth – once or twice a week is quite sufficient. When the puppy is teething, leave its mouth alone, and when you are at training classes, ask the trainer to refrain from looking at its mouth, until the dog is confident with it surroundings. A bad experience with a sore mouth may give it an aversion to having its mouth examined. The puppy should be trained to stand while its teeth are being examined. Lots of handlers put their dog at the 'sit', so that it cannot escape. This really means that it has not been trained properly – and you will have to set it up all over again. If the puppy tries to walk backwards while being examined, have someone stand behind it, so that it learns that if it does this, it bumps into something and still cannot escape. Lots of praise is important during this training. If the examination is carried out gently and correctly, the dog feels comfortable, and accepts the procedure without fuss. The main rules are:
1. Do not cover its nose.   2. Do not cover its eyes.
3. Do not straddle its back, covering its entire head with your body.
4. Do not force its mouth open.
 Handlers make all these mistakes. They also stick their heads in the way of the judge's vision. The dog should also be accustomed to having its mouth examined by a stranger. Breed specialists usually ask the handler to show the mouth, but some all-rounders like to look themselves."

The correct procedure for showing the mouth.

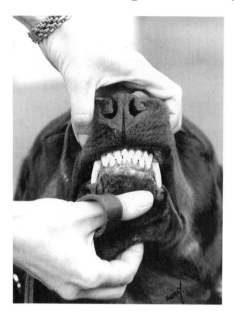

Stage 1: Place your left hand over the muzzle, thumb on one side and fingers on the other. Hold the skin just under the lower jaw with the right hand, say "teeth", and gently pull the the upper and lower lips back so that the front teeth are exposed. The nostrils are clear, and the dog can see what is going on.
Russell Fine Art.

Stage 2: Presenting the side teeth. Some judges may wish to count the teeth, so it is important that every tooth is visible. Do not obscure the teeth with your fingers.
Russell Fine Art.

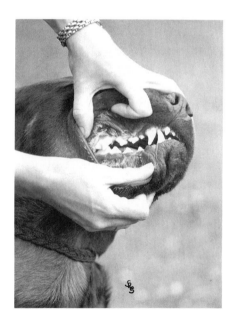

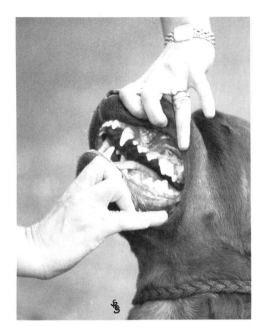

Stage 3: Show the other side, using all of your fingers. If the dog is panting, all the better. It is easier for the judge to view the whole of the lower jaw and see the very small pre molars, which are situated just behind the canine teeth in both jaws. Liz usually drops her lead and stands on it, which leaves both hands free, or she holds the lead high up under the dog's throat and threads it through the right hand. You should always keep your dog firmly under control during this procedure, and never put the dog at risk. If you are nervous, then this transmits down the lead and makes the dog nervous.

Russell Fine Art.

This shows the wrong way to show your dog's teeth. The dog is being straddled by the handler, and he cannot breathe or see. The finger-nails are hurting his gums and he must feel totally claustrophobic – no wonder he is struggling – but it is surprising how frequently handlers subject their dogs to this sort of treatment in the show ring.
Russell Fine Art.

Movement

This shows the side gait, with the handler and dog moving in unison. The handler's elbows are tucked in, and she is encouraging the dog to keep his head up by small jerks on the lead, and then allowing it to slacken, so that he moves on a loose lead.
Hartley

The positioning of the dog and handler, moving away from the judge.
Hartley

Handler and dog returning to the judge.

Hartley

Moving a dog in the show ring is an important lesson to learn. Liz normally uses a leather lead to show males, but Fantasa Crimson Cavalier is quite headstrong and has the habit of dropping his head to the floor. When he is baited he loses concentration very easily, especially when the judge comes to him for his examination. He wags his tail at the judge, and leaves Liz standing while smothering the judge with wet kisses! She therefore uses a nylon collar and a very short lead, which has a leather handle, and this enables her to keep the dog where she wants him. She can guide his head easily, and move him in the way she wants to. A good handler moves with the dog's natural stride. Look down at the dog's front movement, and match your foot placement with its front feet.

COMMON HANDLING FAULTS

The handler is standing too close. The dog's head is looking skywards, and the back legs are tucked under. If a handler constantly ends up with the dog looking like this, use a mirror to see how dreadful it looks.
Russell Fine Art.

This shows a puppy going through the 'legs and wings' stage. He is standing slightly 'ten to two' in front, as he has not yet dropped in brisket. Lifting the front by the shoulder only accentuates the problem. This method should only be used on adults with a perfect front.
Russell Fine Art.

Front set too wide.
Russell Fine Art.

Rear lifted by the stifle,
and set too wide.
Russell Fine Art.

This shows incorrect collar placement. The chain is being pulled too tightly and is spoiling the line of the neck. The dog has not been trained correctly, and the handler does not have the confidence to allow the dog to stand on his own.
                    Russell Fine Art.

The dog is over-stretched and is in what is often known as the 'rocking horse' position.
                    Russell Fine Art.

Ch. Chesara Dark Rachel showing correct show stance.   *Pearce.*

   Not everyone will find that the methods Liz has illustrated are the most suitable for themselves. However, she has proved in the show ring that her methods work and are successful. We feel that there is much to be gained from an understanding of her handling style, and we are sure that many handlers could benefit from studying it.

   We now move on to the role of the judge. We have devoted a considerable amount of space to exhibiting, but, in our opinion, that is as it should be. You should only contemplate entering the ring as a judge after many years of success as a breeder and exhibitor. In other words, you should prove that you have knowledge, experience and an eye for a dog, before you start to inflict your opinions on others. Far too often we meet people who consider that, because they have owned one dog who has done a small amount of winning, they are fully qualified to judge. The British system allows any individual to judge, regardless of their experience. The only criterion is that a club organising a show has to invite you. This means that if you have a friend who is secretary to a show society, you stand a good chance of receiving an invitation, especially if you are in a position to offer one in return. In Britain, it is often asked why a championship show secretary almost invariably finishes up as an all-rounder, judging Best in Show, and other prestigious appointments. We have yet to hear of the converse happening, where a famous and able all-rounder becomes a championship show secretary! The only occasions when a judge is required to satisfy the Kennel Club of their ability is if K.C. Challenge Certificates are on offer. On these occasions, the K.C. asks a prospective judge to provide details of their experience in the breed, and makes a decision based on this experience and any other factors that the committee considers relevant. The system works reasonably well, and bearing in mind the very large number of shows in Britain, it is probably the only way of providing the quantity of judges required. It does, however, allow a percentage of poor judges to officiate at the lower level of Open Shows, and it can be abused at the higher Championship Show level by the undue use of influence – especially as many of the members of the decision-making K.C. committee are also judges and show secretaries. We have long felt that the jet aircraft has had a detrimental effect on the quality of British judges. In the past, a visit to the far side of the world meant a journey of several weeks by ship and a similar time for the return. Today, the same journey is a only a matter of hours. As a result, it is possible to have a very enjoyable trip around the world, with all expenses paid, accommodation at top hotels, and V.I.P. status, in return for judging a number of dog shows. Because shows paying for such judges like to obtain the best value for their money, it is an advantage for such judges to have Kennel Club approval to judge as many breeds as possible at Championship level. This results in judges using all available means to qualify for the maximum number of breeds.

By now you have probably decided that we have a rather jaundiced opinion of many judges. This is correct, but we would hasten to add that there are a large number of judges, both breed specialists and all-rounders, who have devoted years of experience and hard work to learning their craft, and who carry out their appointments with knowledge and integrity. As far as this book is concerned, we are dealing with the question of being a Rottweiler breed specialist judge. In our opinion, this is quite enough to start off with. However, the message is the same. You should spend many years acquiring knowledge of the breed before you aspire to judge it. You should also establish quite clearly in your own mind your motives for wishing to judge. There is only one right motive – you genuinely believe that you have such a thorough knowledge of the breed that, when you judge, your decisions will be both correct, and to the benefit of the breed. In fact, your own opinion of your ability is not sufficient; the same opinion should be held by others, including those who will exhibit under you. If among your reasons for judging you include such thoughts as: 'if Mr A. judges, why shouldn't I?' or 'judging will help me to win when I exhibit' or 'I can sell my puppies for a higher price because I am a judge', then we suggest that you are not yet ready to judge the breed, and may never be ready to do so.

Assuming that you have the right motivation and the necessary knowledge, we suggest that you make your debut with a small number of classes at an Open or similar small show. In any case, it is unlikely that you will be asked to start with anything more ambitious. This first show is not the occasion for you to set the entire breed to rights by trying to prove that all the other judges have been crooks or idiots, and that, at last, the world has an able judge in the middle of the ring. It may be your opinion, but it is unlikely to be supported by everybody else. You may be nervous on your first appointment. We can think of a number of able people who delayed accepting invitations to judge, because they were too shy to accept, or because they were not confident in their own ability. At the end of the day, these people have made better judges than those who have rushed in at the first opportunity. Nervousness need not be a problem if you are confident in your own ability, and if you stick to one simple rule: walk into the ring, examine each dog thoroughly, and then place the dogs in the order of merit which you believe they deserve. You may not be entirely right, but if all judges had the same opinions, there would be no more dog shows. If you follow this rule, you can leave the ring at the end of the day with a clear conscience, and with the satisfaction of a job done to the best of your ability. If, however, you look at the dogs in front of you and try and take into account that A is by your stud dog, B is owned by your best friend, C is handled by next week's judge, and D is bred by your worst enemy, then you you may be sure that you will make a disastrous mess of your judging. Contrary to some people's opinions, judging appointments are not given as an opportunity to repay your debts or to work off old scores. You will have to make decisions about dogs that carry your bloodlines, or that are owned by your close friends. Some judges will tell you that they did not give an award to a dog which they considered to be the best, because it was either owned by a friend or carried the judge's bloodlines. In our opinion, it is just as dishonest to withhold an award from a deserving dog for these reasons, as it is to give an award to a poor dog for the same reasons.

Now let us look at the actual mechanics of judging. When you are dealing with a short-coated breed like a Rottweiler, it is possible to see all the details of the dog's conformation while standing two or three feet away from it. You will have to examine its mouth in detail, you may wish to run your hands over the coat to check its texture, you will have to check males for entirety, and you may wish to feel the shoulders and the musculature of the hindquarters. There is no reason to run your hands all over the dog as if you had been given a lump of putty and told to mould a dog with it. If you cannot see how the dog is made from a distance, then you really should not be judging it. Some all-rounders will tell you that unless you go through a long routine of handling every part of the dog, the exhibitor will not believe that you have judged it properly. This really sums it up. Excessive handling is nothing more than an act to show the exhibitor and the ringside that you are judging the dog. With a Rottweiler, over-handling is often counter-productive. Even the steadiest Rott can take exception to being pushed and pulled for no apparent reason. It is not just coincidence that the judges who get bitten most frequently, are those who over-handle.

Be gentle with beginners, both canine and human. Remember that there was a time when you and your young puppy were both entering the ring for the first time, and you were both apprehensive about what was going to happen. Rude and brusque behaviour can put a new exhibitor off dog showing for life, and rough handling a puppy can ruin the prospects of a promising youngster. There is no benefit in forcing a nervous youngster to be handled. It is far better to give it, and its owner, an understanding, kind word, and hope that they will try again when they have gained confidence. Equally, you will not gain any applause if you persist, in spite of roars of rage, in examining the teeth of a large unruly male, who has a hopeless handler. It is far better to quietly leave him out of your placings than to run the risk of getting bitten.

When you judge, you should be confident – and hopefully that confidence is apparent to the ring-side. One way of giving this desirable impression is in your control of the ring. Make it clear to your steward where you want your dogs lined up, where you want any dog that you have seen in a previous class placed, which part of the ring you wish kept clear for movement, and finally, where you will line up your winners. This last directive is most important. There are always several different ways you can line up your first, second, third placings, and nothing looks worse than placing the line in a different position in the ring for each class. Apart from looking untidy, you can confuse both the exhibitors, your steward and the ringside. You could even achieve the ridiculous situation of muddling your steward to such an extent that he gives the prize cards out in the wrong order. Remember, if this happens, it is your fault.

Good judges of Rottweilers can be of great value to the breed. We hope that you will aspire to such a position, and that you will remember that, as a judge, you carry great responsibility for Rottweilers, and for their future.

Chapter Ten

THE ROTTWEILER
IN THE USA

As in Britain, the Rottweiler has had an enormous success in the U.S.A. In sheer numbers of dogs, owners, clubs, and even in the volume of literature – either original or translated – the American Rottweiler scene is the biggest in the world. At the time of writing, the U.S.A. has some fifty-four breed clubs from California to New England, including three in Canada, all under the overall umbrella of the American Rottweiler Club. The ARC is sometimes described as the parent club, although this particular parent was born, or perhaps we should say reborn, after the birth of some of its more long-established offspring. The first American Rottweiler Club was formed in 1948. It was short-lived, possibly because of the problems involved for any one club, in those early days, of attempting to serve a membership scattered over an area as vast as the U.S.A.

Ignoring for the moment the original ARC, the first club to become firmly established was the Colonial Rottweiler Club, mainly covering the eastern seaboard, formed in 1956; this was followed by the Medallion Rottweiler Club in the middle west in 1959, and the Golden State Rottweiler Club serving California in 1962. All of the breed clubs are autonomous bodies running their own affairs, although answerable to the American Kennel Club. It was an imaginative move by delegates from the established clubs to create the present American Rottweiler Club in 1971. This club has no direct authority over the breed clubs, but its policy can be influenced by submissions and representation. Its great advantage is that American Rottweiler owners can speak with one powerful voice. The ARC provides a wide range of aid and facilities to other clubs and owners. Apart from its officers and directors, it lists no fewer than twenty sub-committees, with functions ranging from Judges Education to Rottweiler Character Testing, and from Financial and Tax Advice to Public Information Representative. The ARC also carries responsibility for revisions to the Breed Standard and their subsequent submission and adoption by the American Kennel Club. As a result, the ARC produces the excellent Illustrated Standard of the Rottweiler, which is incorporated in this book.

The ARC sets out to try and ensure that it members maintain the highest possible standards of ethics and behaviour in all matters affecting Rottweilers. It lays down a Statement of Principles and Practices, which has obviously been very carefully thought out, and if it is complied with, it will be of great assistance in eliminating many of the malpractices which do so much harm to Rottweilers and dogs in general. Its membership application asks a long list of searching questions, which contrasts favourably with the attitude of many breed clubs who are prepared to take virtually anyone as a member provided that they pay their dues. Bearing in mind that the Rottweiler in the U.S.A. is suffering from the same sort of misuse by the wrong sort of people as it is in Britain, which is creating similar demands for punitive legislation against the breed, it is vital that the breed clubs do all in their power to maintain the breed's good name.

The American Kennel Club first registered a Rottweiler in 1931. This was a bitch imported from Germany by August Knecht. He followed this with a dog, Arras v. Gerbermuhle, and bred a litter from this pair which were duly registered at the AKC. Nothing much happened after this until after World War Two. In the thirteen years from 1931 a total of 93 dogs were registered. Many of the pioneers during this period had emigrated from Europe bringing their knowledge and their dogs with them. As in Britain, many of the early successes of the breed were in the working and obedience ring. The foundation in the late fifties and early sixties of the three main clubs, located right across the country, reflects the rising interest in the breed. It was at exactly the same time that interest started to grow in Britain. In 1980 the

AKC registered 4701 Rottweilers. The comparable British figure was 1298. By 1985 the AKC figure was 22,886, and in 1989 it had reached the enormous figure of 51,291, putting the Rottweiler in number one place in the Working Group. British readers should note that the AKC splits the Working Group into Working and Herding, with German Shepherds in the latter. In 1979 Joan Klem, writing in the Medallion Rottweiler Club Anniversary Book, said: "We do not need any more quantity, but we should strive for more quality." Writing a decade later, when the figure had increased 1400 per cent, she echoes the problem that we have highlighted in this book, pointing out that the Rottweiler's good qualities have promoted its popularity, but unfortunately, popularity tends to cause the demise of the very qualities which made it so popular. While the total of responsible members may have grown in proportion to the total number of dogs, it is likely that the numbers of irresponsible owners will have also increased. While a small number of bad owners may not present a major problem to a breed, irresponsible or criminal ownership by a large number of people will quickly attract the attentions of both government and the anti-dog lobby. In dealing with attacks on specific breeds, or on dogs in general, British owners look with envy on their American counterparts for the way that the American Kennel Club comes out fighting against any form of unfair legislation against dogs. The idea of a lawyer, briefed by the British Kennel Club, standing up in court and fighting a local ordinance placing unreasonable restrictions on dogs, is totally unbelievable – although we are told it is quite a common occurrence in the States.

Understandably, the U.S.A. has produced a considerable number of well-known names in the breed. Many of them have become internationally respected, wherever Rottweilers are popular. One family can almost be described as founding a Rottweiler dynasty. Pat Rademacher bought his first Rottweiler in 1945. Together with his sister, Joan Klem, they founded the Rodsdens kennel, which after forty-five years still holds a prominent position in the world of Rottweilers. Joan Klem was a founder member of the Medallion Rottweiler Club, and has been its president since 1979. A glance at the current list of club officers will show that another generation of Rademachers are also serving the breed. Rodsdens have imported a large number of German-bred dogs; the most famous is the dog that must be rated as one of the all-time greats – Int. Ch. Harras von Sofienbusch. Born in December 1957, he gained the title of Bundessieger for three successive years, 1960/61/62, in Germany before being sold to Rodsdens. Those who knew him will admit that, like many top stud dogs, he was an extremely tough character, a fact that probably inhibited the extent to which he was shown in the States. However, as a stud force he had a major effect on the breed, exerting an influence which still continues.

Int. Ch. Am. Ch. Harras v. Sofienbusch SchH1. Bundessieger 1960, 61, 62. Imported and owned by Rademacher-Klem.

Clara Hurley and Michael Grossman's Am. Ch. Nelson v h Brabantpark. In 1989 and 1990, he made American breed history, defeating more Rottweilers than any other dog in the country.

No record of American Rottweiler personalities would be complete without mention of Muriel Freeman, first president of the re-formed American Rottweiler Club, a founder member of the Colonial Rottweiler Club, and perhaps most important of all, the person largely responsible for establishing the Orthopedic Foundation for Animals as the body for the X-ray screening of Rottweilers as a means of controlling hip dysplasia. She became president of the O.F.A. in 1983. In many countries where the Rottweiler has been successful, the breed has also produced a number of determined and dedicated women experts. Often small in stature but huge in personality, these ladies have pushed the breed in the direction which they felt it should go, frequently against the opposition of lesser mortals who were often male. There has frequently seemed to be an affinity and understanding between such ladies and Rottweilers, which must be the envy of those who lack their spirit. Muriel Freeman must be numbered amongst these ladies who have done much for the breed.

One of the major services that the U.S.A. has performed for the English-speaking section of the Rottweiler world is the translation and publication of many books on the breed, written in German, Dutch or Finnish. Starting with the English edition of Hans Korn and going on through a number of paper-bound copies of works that were originally written in German, to translations from the Dutch of the work of D. Chardet and from the Finnish of J. A. U. Yrjola and Elvi Tikka, our library shelves contain many treasures for which we can thank the Americans. Much of this work has been done by Clara Hurley and her Powderhorn Press in California. She was one of the first members of the Golden State Rottweiler Club, and has another claim to fame as the creator of the Rottweiler Registry or Biodex. This records the HD status of Rottweilers under the O.F.A. scheme, and provides breeders with similar information to that given by Malcolm Willis in Britain. In 1989 and 1990 Clara Hurley's Dutch import Champion Nelson vh Brabantpark was the number one Rottweiler in the U.S.A., defeating more Rottweilers than any other Rottweiler in the history of the breed in America. By highlighting a personality from each of the three original American breed clubs, we have tried to show how the early pioneers have continued to serve the breed, giving it the benefit of their knowledge and experience from the beginning up to the present day.

The sheer numerical size of the breed in the States, means that in terms of facilities and collective knowledge, the Rottweiler is remarkably well served. It is probably true to say that the average American breeder has more disposable income to spend on his hobby than his British counterpart, and this can be seen from the number of highly-priced imports that have come from Germany and elsewhere. However, a study of Rottweilers in the U.S.A. will show that there are many breeders making good use of the stock available to breed excellent Rottweilers, rather than relying on imports. American breed clubs do all in their power to encourage their members to breed from sound stock, especially with regard to hip dysplasia. However, like Britain, they lack the final power of enforcement – refusing to register stock that has not been X-rayed. Both countries must envy the German approach, whereby the breed club is able to ban the breeding of stock that has an unacceptable level of HD. While the American and German systems of assessment for HD achieve the desired object, we consider that the British system of hip-scoring gives the maximum amount of useful information to breeders.

America and Britain differ in their methods for making up Champions, and, having judged under both systems, we think that both have their good and their bad points. The geographical size of the U.S.A. means that professional handlers need to be employed if a dog is to be campaigned in the show ring, and this is obviously an added expense for a kennel to bear. Although professional handlers are fairly common in a few breeds in Britain, they are never seen in the Rottweiler ring. The American points system, and the separation of Champions into a class of their own, means that up-and-coming young dogs do not have to compete against Champions in order to gain their points. Under the British system, three Challenge Certificates awarded under three different judges are required before a dog can claim the title of Champion. Whenever Challenge Certificates are on offer, the classes are open to all dogs – including Champions – and to win, the dog must beat all entrants. On one occasion, Judy judged a class in another breed, which included twenty-four Champions, and it obviously takes a very good newcomer to beat that sort of competition. At times, this means that dogs who are worthy of their titles are held back. Cases are on record of dogs winning twenty or more Reserve Challenge Certificates, because they are repeatedly beaten by one or two outstanding dogs. Equally, it could be argued that the American system of separating Champions means that it is an easier task to acquire the fifteen points required to become a Champion. We believe the British system could be modified by allowing, for instance, three Reserve Challenge Certificates to count as one Challenge Certificate, probably with a requirement that the dog must win at least two full certificates.

American Rottweiler owners are obviously aware of the problems suffered by any breed which achieves enormous popularity. The initial reaction may be one of pride that the breed you love has become a success, but your pleasure can soon turn to regret at the damage done by commercialism and ownership by unsuitable people. We fear that the massive popularity of the Rottweiler in the U.S.A. could lead to many problems for the breed, as it has done in Britain. We can only hope that the breed clubs and their members will succeed in overcoming such difficulties.

Chapter Eleven

ROTTWEILERS OVERSEAS

The worldwide popularity of the Rottweiler during the last thirty years has meant that there are few countries, where the inhabitants are interested in dogs, that do not contain at least a few specimens of the breed. Space prohibits us covering all of them, and we must therefore limit ourselves to those countries we have visited, and those where information is freely available.

While it is true to say that in many of the countries where the Rottweiler has become popular, part of the appeal has been the ability of the breed to protect its owner and family, this does not detract from the fact that in such countries there are many enthusiastic owners who admire the breed for its overall qualities, and its ability to be a part of the family as well as its protector. Visiting such countries we have seen many excellent Rottweilers, kept under ideal conditions by owners who have made themselves knowledgeable about the breed, and who have spent a considerable amount of time and money to overcome the difficulties caused by geographic isolation, cost, financial restrictions and quarantine regulations. In many of these countries we have been impressed by the enthusiasm and by the desire for further knowledge shown by Rottweiler lovers.

Bearing in mind the enthusiasm and not inconsiderable knowledge that exists in many of the countries that have only a relatively small Rottweiler population, we have always been surprised at the modest way in which these enthusiasts deny themselves the opportunity to judge their breed. They very generously spend large sums of money to bring in judges from the U.S.A., Britain and Europe, while at the same time making little effort to encourage the development of their own 'home grown' product. This attitude is often supported by local Kennel Club policy, which makes it extremely difficult for such people to gain judging experience. While we are not suggesting that the local judges should immediately start judging Championship shows, we are certain that more could be done, starting with events such as matches, as they are known in Britain – small informal affairs where the dogs are matched in pairs. The best of each pair goes on to be paired again until the decision lies between a final pair. The winner of this pair become Best in Match. Such matches have long been recognised in Britain as a training ground both for new judges and for young dogs. No great harm is done if the judge gets it wrong, and the events are both social and instructive.

AUSTRALIA

Excluding the U.S.A., Britain and the rest of Europe, the Rottweiler is probably more strongly established in Australia than anywhere else in the world, with the possible exception of South Africa. It is one of the small ironies of history that the man who made the first attempt to establish the breed there, was the veterinary surgeon Captain Roy-Smith, who is also in the history books as the man who set out to re-establish the breed in Britain after World War Two. Roy-Smith did not have a lot of luck in either venture. His British imports had little effect on the breed, with the exception of Rintelna the Bombardier, bred from his second imported bitch. His Australian imports, taken out there by him in 1962, fared little better. The first litter were put down for lack of suitable buyers, with the exception of one, Rintelna the Empress, who went to a former Dutch police officer who knew Rottweilers. A second mating produced three puppies, two of which went to Douglas Mummery. The bitch, Rintelna the Fatale, went on to produce a number of litters. Roy-Smith's Rintelna stock did, in fact, produce three Champions; but this statement must be considered against the fact that there were virtually no other Rottweilers in the country and the Australian system allowed dogs to win Challenge Certificates without any competition. Sadly, neither Roy-Smith, nor his stock, survived long enough to play a significant part in the story of the Rottweiler in Australia.

The two men who played the major part in establishing the Rottweiler in Australia were Douglas Mummery and Colonel Jim Pettengell. Mr Mummery imported Pilgrimsway Loki, a son of Rintelna the Bombardier, from the U.K. in 1963. Loki did a lot for the breed's reputation in Australia, siring two Champions and providing Jim Pettengell with his first Rottweiler, Heatherglen Chablis Khan. In 1967 Jim Pettengell imported Chesara Dark Impression from our kennels, and to quote her owner: "She left an indelible impression on the breed, and for many years most of the leading Rottweilers in Australia had her name in their pedigrees." In 1987 Jim Pettengell imported a young dog from Germany via the U.K., who was the 1986 Youth Sieger. This was Graf von Gruntenblick, who, in our opinion, was one of the best young Rottweilers that the Germans had ever allowed to leave Germany. During his stay in England, Jim allowed the dog to be used at stud, although this had to be limited to the one month between coming out of quarantine and his departure to Australia. Unfortunately, few people in England took advantage of this very generous offer, and the opportunity to acquire his bloodlines in the U.K. was largely lost. At the time of writing, we are lucky enough to own a son of his, who reflects many of his father's qualities, including his excellent temperament. Graf quickly became a Champion in Australia and should play a major part in the future of the Rottweiler in that country.

NEW ZEALAND

Like so many other countries, Rottweilers were late arrivals in New Zealand, and the first one came from Australia in 1970. However, by the mid-eighties there were several hundred, with nearly four hundred registered in 1984. By the late eighties the breed was strong, both in quantity and quality. Much of the present stock is home-bred out of U.K. imports, with others coming in from Australia. Faced with the problems of distance from Europe and quarantine, the New Zealanders have done well in breeding good Rottweilers from the stock that they have available – a success story that could well be emulated by other countries with similar problems.

One of the attractive aspects of the dog show scene in New Zealand is the 'laid back' attitude of show organisers and exhibitors. Few exhibitors have the intense desire to win at all costs that mars so much of the dog show world elsewhere. Equally, the show organisers do not spend most of the show worrying as to whether they will be in trouble with their Kennel Club for some unwitting breach of regulations. The attitude of exhibitors is especially commendable because the majority of the show wins are made by a relatively small percentage of top dogs. This does not stop the bulk of the exhibitors turning out with their Rottweilers, even though it is almost certain that they will not be in the cards. Show organisation is helped by the fact that there is almost always a senior Kennel Club member at the show, willing to advise and help, and even lend a hand with the chores.

Larry was invited to judge in New Zealand and has happy memories of a 6a.m. start, to drive to a show at Rotorua. With about a hundred miles to travel, a convoy of dog cars, many of them towing specially designed dog trailers, drove through the lovely countryside and small towns, with the only other traffic being the numerous giant stainless steel milk tankers collecting their daily load from the dairy farms. On arrival at the show ground, the committee went to work. One made sure that the horse trough was filled with cans of beer being cooled for later in the day. Another started the barbecue, while the rest put up the ring and got the show going. What more could anyone ask than to watch Rottweilers and their owners enjoying themselves, surrounded by magnificent scenery, a hot sun shining from a clear blue sky, while drinking cold beer and eating a barbecued steak? This, we decided, was dog showing as it should be!

The New Zealand system requires a dog to win eight Challenge Certificates before it becomes a champion. This must be weighed against the fact that it is possible for a Challenge Certificate to be won by a dog that is the only specimen of the breed entered at the show. Until the system was explained to him, Larry was more than a little surprised when he was told that the New Zealand-bred dog, N.Z. Ch. Rangirahi Silent Sentry, who he had just made Best in Show at the 1988 Breed Club Championship Show, had won eighty Challenge Certificates. The dog was still a worthy Champion, and on that day had gained his award competing against a large entry of his own kind.

New Zealand supports two Rottweiler breed clubs, one based in Auckland and the other in Wellington. The vast majority of owners carry out regular training with their Rotts, and the dogs are very much part of the family.

SOUTH AFRICA

Compared with many countries, the Rottweiler made a relatively early appearance in South Africa. It was imported in small numbers in the late thirties, but numbers were negligible up to 1970. From 1956 to 1973 the average registrations were about six dogs per year, with the bulk of these coming towards the end of the period. However, in the mid-seventies interest in the breed began to increase rapidly and registrations began to run in excess of 600 per year. By 1979 they were running at over 2,000, rising to a peak of over 4000 in 1983. From 1975 until 1983 the South African Rottweiler registrations were comfortably greater than those in the U.K.

In South Africa the Rottweiler's ability to live with the family, but also to act as its protector, contributed greatly to its popularity. This trend has continued; many dogs live in rural areas, leading what can be described as the ideal life for a Rottweiler, combining duties as a guard and as a working dog on a farm – the tasks for which the breed was originally created. While breeders and show enthusiasts may regret the loss of good quality dogs to the show world, there can be no doubt that such dogs, playing a useful role in the community, are of great importance to the breed. South Africa's links with Holland, and the ties that the region formerly known as South West Africa has with Germany – coupled with the absence of quarantine restrictions – have meant that much of the stock has come direct from Europe, unlike those countries which have to import from, or via, the U.K.

Our own first contact with South Africa came as a result of a telephone call one morning from a Mr E. M. Gant of Cape Town. The previous day he had been in Denmark, where he had come across a magnificent dog, lying in front of a roaring log fire, in the hunting lodge where he was staying. He learnt that this was a Rottweiler; he had never seen the breed before, or even heard of it. However, it appeared to be love at first sight, as his first action on arriving in London was to make enquiries about acquiring a Rottweiler. One aspect of his business was cattle, and he was a man who knew and admired top quality livestock of all kinds. In the autumn of 1967 he took Chesara Dark Tabor back to South Africa. This was a son of our Dutch import Luther, and for many years afterwards we received an annual card showing Tabor enjoying life on the rolling lawns in front of the Gant home.

Jann Cornelius did much to establish the breed in South Africa, especially in the Durban area. Her prefix of Arcadia came from the P&O liner of that name, where she met her husband, a merchant navy officer. When he left the merchant navy he became a shipping agent in Angola, and at this stage, in 1968, Jann obtained Chesara Dark Zorro from our kennels. Soon afterwards they all moved to Durban, where over a number of years Jann added several more Chesara bitches to her kennel, including Chesara Dark Ilenka, whose name appears on many South African pedigrees and who was the dam of several champions. A considerable amount of the credit for the remarkable increase in registrations from 1975 onwards must go to Dudley Bennett, who founded the Rottweiler Working and Breeding Association in 1973, and is now president of the South African Rottweiler Club, and to Jann Cornelius, who formed a club for breeders in the Natal area. It is likely that the existence of clubs for breeders acted as an encouragement for owners to register their dogs. Rottweilers who had been living in happy obscurity became part of the official statistics. Dudley Bennett's Tankerville kennel is established as a major force in South Africa.

THE CARIBBEAN

As in so many other parts of the world, the need for a house dog as a protector has meant that the large guard breeds are in a majority in Jamaica, Trinidad and Tobago, and Barbados. The entries at shows for Rottweilers, German Shepherds and Dobermanns can be quite substantial, compared to other breeds, which often consist of just one specimen. Looking back at our records, we find that we first sent a Rottweiler to St.Vincent in the Caribbean in 1968. A second, Chesara Dark Raul, went to Trinidad in 1970, and the following year Clyde Fisher took Chesara Lady Macbeth and Chesara Dark Warrior to Jamaica and made them both into Champions. He subsequently imported several more Rottweilers, and he went on to found the Rottweiler Club of Jamaica and did a lot to establish the breed there.

The Rottweiler Club of Trinidad and Tobago is a fairly new club with a number of enthusiastic members. Clubs such as this and in Jamaica go to a lot of expense to bring in overseas judges, and they take endless trouble to ensure that such judges enjoy their stay in these lovely islands. Larry has fond memories of consuming considerable quantities of what seems to be Trinidad's national drink – rum and coke – while admiring the Trinidad Cricket Club ground. The problem was that although it was only midnight in Port of Spain, it was five o'clock in the morning British-time, and Larry had flown out that day! Because of the cost involved and the relatively small entries, shows in the Caribbean accept a considerable amount of sponsorship, and you have to get used to hearing the public address system broadcasting commercials and thanks to sponsors, while you are judging. Although this may offend some people used to the British system, the hard fact is that without such generous support there would be no shows.

The Caribbean islands have a considerable number of keen and knowledgeable Rottweiler enthusiasts. Although they have problems of climate and disease, which those of us living in more temperate regions do not have to cope with, their dogs are kept in excellent condition and are obviously well cared for and much loved.

GERMANY

Any review of the Rottweiler must inevitably start, continue and finish with Germany as the focal point. In every aspect of the breed, the part played by

Germany is paramount. Throughout the world, Rottweiler lovers acknowledge the breed's debt to its country of origin. However, we do not intend to go into any great detail of the Rottweiler in Germany. For a start, we would consider it to be presumptuous on the part of comparative newcomers to the Rottweiler scene. More importantly, the Rottweiler is extremely well documented in Germany. From Hans Korn to the present day, Germany has produced a long list of authors who have studied the breed and written about it to the benefit of the rest of the world.

In 1969 Germany founded the International Federation for Rottweiler Friends (IFR). The first congress of the IFR was held in Essen in May 1969. This excellent scheme, aimed at providing an opportunity for Rottweiler enthusiasts from all over the world to meet and exchange ideas and knowledge of the breed, has, for a number of reasons, failed to develop into anything more than a forum for the friendly exchange of opinions. At the outset there were those, particularly in Germany, who hoped that it would provide a means whereby Germany could exert actual control of the breed throughout the world. The F.C.I. "country of origin" rule, giving such countries precedence in matters affecting their native breeds, helped to encourage this hope. The man who held the position of Chief Breed Warden of the ADRK for many years was the late Friedrich Berger. There can be no doubt that Berger would have liked to use the IFR to impose his views on the breed. Bearing in mind that Berger had an enormous knowledge, love and understanding of the Rottweiler, it is possible to argue that this would have been to the benefit of the breed. However, Friedrich, great Rottweiler man that he was, could hardly be called a diplomat, and most of us would consider that the breed is better served by allowing a reasonable diversion of opinion. Breeders, especially in Britain and the U.S.A., are fiercely independent and have proved for many years that they are capable of producing good stock by their own methods. The British and American Kennel Clubs are both self-governing, so this meant that breeders from both countries had to inform the IFR Congress that, while they were very happy, and indeed anxious, to exchange views and opinions and to listen to advice, they could not, under the rules of their respective Kennel Clubs, submit to the jurisdiction of any other body. This point of view was understood and accepted, and the IFR has continued not only as a forum to exchange knowledge, but as an opportunity to meet old friends from many countries.

For many years now the Allgemeiner Deutscher Rottweiler Klub has pursued a wise and benevolent policy of cooperation with other countries, with the prime aim being the welfare of the breed, coupled with the acceptance that breeders all over the world have the same aim. It is highly unlikely that any one will ever again make a speech on the lines of the one made by Friedrich Berger to the 1972 IFR congress, when he virtually accused British and American judges of ruining the breed in their respective countries. The rest of Europe, quite rightly, looks to Germany for leadership in Rottweiler affairs while at the same time retaining their independence. Many judges from these countries qualify under the German rules and are then accepted to judge in Germany. Conversely, judges from Germany officiate outside Germany to the benefit of the country concerned.

HOLLAND

Our association with Rottweilers spanning thirty years has meant for us an equally long association with Holland and the Dutch, and we have grown to love the country and have made many friends there. Three out of our four imports, all carefully chosen to fill a particular need, have come from Dutch kennels, and we have found that Dutch breeders are very anxious that any stock that they send abroad should be worthy specimens of the breed.

The Rottweiler has a long history in Holland – the earliest records go back before 1914. The breed has always had a strong following, and as in Germany, Dutch breeders take their responsibilities very seriously. There have been, and still are, a number of famous and successful kennels in Holland. These include the Brabantpark prefix owned by Mrs A. Huijskens, and the Triomfator owned by Miss E. C. Gruter. Back in the mid-sixties, the dog Champion Baldur v. Habennichts, owned by Mrs Teneke Boltjesthe – then chairman of the Netherlands Rottweiler Club – charmed us both with his type and with his character. As a result, we imported one of his sons, Ch. Chesara Luther, who became the first male Rottweiler Champion in Britain,

Much of the early work on hip dysplasia was done by the late Dr. van de Velden at Utrecht University, where Rottweilers were used for the study. While this work was of major importance, it had the effect of suggesting that H.D. was of particular importance in Rottweilers, simply because more was known about the condition in the breed than in any other. At the same time, the Dutch breed club, acting very responsibly, considered that no dog showing signs of H.D. should be bred from. This meant that for a while it was difficult to find a sire that would be approved.

Among other claims to fame, Holland holds a high place in our esteem as the home of the author one of the most charming books on the breed, *My Friend Rik* by Jan van Rheenen – a copy has been on our bookshelf from the very beginning.

SWEDEN

Like other European countries, Swedish Rottweiler owners have maintained close links with Germany. The first Rottweiler in the country was registered in 1914, and the first dog to exert a major influence on the breed was imported in 1921. During the ten years from 1980 to 1989 registrations rose gradually, and are now running at about 600 per year – a figure to be envied by countries such as the U.S.A. and Britain that are currently wrestling with the problems of annual registration figures running into multi-thousands.

Sweden is fortunate in having an extremely active and supportive Kennel Club, which celebrated its Centennial Year in 1989. The Rottweiler Club (AFR) was founded in 1968. An internationally known figure in Rottweilers is Mrs Gerd Hyden, who has been described as the unofficial breed warden for some forty years. Both she and her husband Sven have been judging the breed since 1940. When we were looking for a stud dog to take the breed forward in Britain in the sixties, we submitted details of our requirements to Mrs Hyden, and as a result, she sent us Ch. Chesara Akilles. He was sired by Int. & Nordic Champion Fandangos Fair Boy, from the famous Swedish Rottweiler kennel of that name.

Sweden has a little-known breed called the Smalandsstovare, which translates as 'Swedish Hare and Foxhound'. The photographs we have seen of the breed show a dog which, to all intents and purposes, looks like a miniature Rottweiler. Furthermore, fifty per cent of the puppies in this breed are born with a stump tail. Any country wrestling with the possibility of a ban on docking could look with interest on the use of this breed as a means of breeding a natural dock. They are also black and tan in colour, and appear to have a similar conformation, other than size, which is 50cms. for males and 46cms. for bitches.

FINLAND

We must confess that it was not until we had been looking at the European Rottweiler scene for several years that we began to realise the importance of Finland, with regard to the breed. A relatively small country, to a certain extent isolated from Western Europe, Finland tends to be overlooked when thinking about Rottweilers. In fact, the country has had a long and successful association with the breed going back to 1923 when the first Rottweiler was registered. The Finnish Rottweiler Club was founded in 1946 and in 1989 there were 2299 members – probably one of the largest memberships in the world apart from the ADRK. As with Sweden, Finland has an effective and active Kennel Club, which was established in 1889. More than one in every hundred Finnish citizens are members of the club, a factor which must allow the club to speak with a strong voice on matters affecting dogs. Two-thirds of all the dogs in Finland are registered with the club. Rottweiler registrations, at the time of writing, are in the region of 600 per year. Finland has twice been the host for the IFR congress, once in 1975 and again in 1988.

Any review of the breed in Finland must include two names that have played a major part in the breed's history. Mr Olavi Pasanen and his wife Maria registered their prefix, vom Heidenmoor, in 1949. At this time Olavi Pasanen was already a founder member of the Rottweiler Club, and for over thirty years the vom Heidenmoor kennel has produced a long line of high quality Rottweilers. The other name in Finnish Rottweiler history is Mr J. A. U. Yrjola. At present the chairman of the Finnish Kennel Club, he has bred Rottweilers since 1952 and has served as the chief breeding advisory counsellor to the Finnish Rottweiler Club for over 25 years. His long experience and knowledge of the breed is reflected in his book *Our Friend the Rottweiler*, published in English by Powderhorn Press of California, which contains a vast amount of vital information and original thinking on rearing, training, judging, and the Breed Standard. This book is a must for anyone with an interest in Rottweilers. Under the title of guidelines for breeders it contains a line which in our opinion should be the motto of all breed clubs and should be carved above the entrance to all Rottweiler kennels: "Try to improve the breed, not to increase it."

Many other countries have strong groups of Rottweiler lovers, such as Norway, Denmark, Belgium and Switzerland. France, Italy and Spain are showing increasing interest, while in North America, Canada has a number of keen owners. In a little over thirty years the Rottweiler has gone from being a breed known only to a relatively small group of enthusiasts in Western Europe and the U.S.A., to a dog loved and admired by owners all over the world.

Chapter Twelve

HEALTH CARE

Dog owners today are well served with regard to the health of their animals. The services of highly trained veterinary surgeons backed up by veterinary colleges undertaking research, and a wide range of pharmaceutical companies producing drugs, are readily available to breeders and owners. Unfortunately, commercial companies do not operate from purely altruistic motives, and their claims and their products must be considered with this in mind, in the same way that the advertising of any product must be assessed. A product may be recommended by your veterinary surgeon in good faith, and in the knowledge that the product is probably effective. However, it may also be preferred because that particular company offers an excellent discount to the vet, or some other incentive. Equally, the days when the majority of veterinary surgeons came from a family background of animal husbandry – probably farming – have sadly gone. The old-time vet who carried his skill in his head and in his hands, and who transported the bulk of his equipment in the back of his car, has been almost entirely replaced by veterinary surgeons who view the profession as a means of making a very good living. There are, of course, many vets who have the basic vocation for the task, combining a love of animals with the scientific skills required to care for them. To be fair, a modern veterinary practice requires considerable expenditure in time and money, not only for the training involved, but in the capital equipment required. X-ray machines, operating theatres and other equipment do not come cheaply, and vets must be forgiven if they, quite rightly, try and recoup this outlay. However, dog owners must be on their guard against the understandable tendency to advise an expensive operation when a zero-cost period of rest would be just as effective, or even the use of a costly course of drugs when a much cheaper and simpler treatment is available. The dog owner must also bear in mind that the operation, while effective, may involve considerable pain and trauma for his dog. None of this should be construed as an excuse to avoid any necessary but expensive treatment, or to use an ineffective or 'quack' cure; but the owner should be aware of the possibility that factors other than the health of his dog may be involved. Having said all this, the fact remains that the vast majority of veterinary surgeons are caring, able, knowledgeable and efficient. Find one that fits this description, and one who is also willing to listen to you, especially if you are experienced in dogs. Having found such a vet, then treasure him or her, pay the bills, and hopefully, the vet will become a friend to both you and your dog. There will inevitably be times when your Rottweiler requires veterinary help, although we hope that these times will be rare.

The relationship between the Rottweiler and the veterinary profession has not always been a happy one. Many Rotts do not take kindly to being handled by strangers, and the belief that they are difficult has, to a certain extent, been encouraged by the teaching at veterinary colleges. You cannot blame a surgeon who does not wish to be bitten, especially as so much of his work is with his hands. However, when you are looking for your ideal vet you should stress that he will be dealing with Rottweilers, and ensure that he is willing to treat them. Some vets are, surprisingly, frightened of all dogs, and unless they intend to specialise in goldfish it is difficult to understand why they entered the profession. Others, as we have mentioned, may have had a wariness of the breed instilled in them during training.

When you have found your ideal veterinary surgeon, then you must play your part by ensuring that your Rott does nothing to damage the mutual relationship between the three of you. We have a firm rule that, as long as our dog is conscious, one of us is present and is holding the sharp end. Working this way we ensure that if anyone is going to get bitten it is one of us, rather than the vet. As a result, neither us nor our vet have ever been bitten during treatment. We also make it quite clear to our Rotts that they must accept what is being done to them without demur, and that the treatment is for their own good. Not all vets are happy to have you present during treatment, preferring to work without an anxious owner breathing down their neck. It is up to you to convince the vet that your way is best, and that you will not be a liability, likely to faint at the first sign of blood.

A number of Rottweilers have died while under a general anaesthetic. As we all know, there is always a slight risk of this happening. The problem is probably aggravated by the veterinary surgeon, aware that he is dealing with a Rottweiler, giving an over-large dose to ensure that the dog does not recover consciousness halfway through the operation. It is also certainly compounded by owners who have an inflated idea of the weight of their dog. Before submitting your Rott to a general anaesthetic you should take the trouble to obtain an accurate figure of its weight.

We do not intend to try and cover all the possible canine illnesses and conditions. There are many excellent books on the subject, and if you have established a good relationship with your vet, he should be your principal adviser on such matters. We therefore intend to cover only those health problems that we have found to be of particular importance in Rottweilers. In general the Rottweiler is a healthy breed. It does not suffer from hereditary conditions brought about by exaggerated breed points, in the way that some breeds are afflicted. The Rottweiler can be described as a sound, basic dog, whose conformation is close to the natural state. It does, however, have certain conditions which are hereditary, although in our opinion these conditions are largely perpetuated by the failure of breeders to take the quite simple steps required to eliminate, or at least reduce, their incidence.

You should be sufficiently knowledgeable to be able to give your vet an accurate description of symptoms, and hopefully the vet will be willing to listen to your suggestions and opinions. After all, you are the one who lives in close proximity to your Rottweiler, and you are therefore in the best position to observe any indications of illness.

OLD AGE

In common with other large breeds, the Rottweiler does not have a long life-span. How often have we wished that our dog could live as long as we do – and preferably not a minute more. Ten years is about the average life expectancy, although many live to eleven or twelve years of age. The record, to the best of our knowledge, is about sixteen. Old age in a Rottweiler manifests itself quite slowly. Your Rott will show little sign of deterioration for the major part of its life. A few grey hairs around the muzzle may show that it is reaching old age. It may become a little stiff in its joints, and it may be more sedate in its movement. It will still wish to retain its dignity and its rightful place in the order of things, so if you keep more than one

Rottweiler you should protect your old ones from being insulted or bullied by the up-and-coming youngsters. Old age should have its privileges. Thankfully, the end, when it does come, can often be quite quick. Most of our Rottweilers have led fit and active lives almost to the end. Some have been enjoying life to the full even during their last day, and have then retired to their beds, settled down comfortably, gone to sleep and not woken up – an end which most of us would envy. Others have suddenly started to show a rapid deterioration and have lasted only a few weeks. The first indication is often a loss of flesh on the head and skull, and the hindquarters lose their firm, rounded muscular strength. All too often this is an indication of cancer, a disease which, sadly, takes the lives of many Rottweilers.

You may be faced with the situation where your dog is obviously suffering pain and incapacity. Your vet may offer you treatment that will postpone the evil day for a few weeks or months, probably with the dog still suffering to some extent. The decision has to be yours, and when you come to make it we would urge you to put aside your own grief and desire to retain the companionship of your Rott for a further short time, and think of the dog. Far too many dogs are allowed to linger on with loss of control and suffering pain because their owner has not got the courage to give their old friend the calm, dignified end that it deserves. An able vet can end a dog's life calmly and painlessly, so that the dog slips quietly into sleep. If you do have to make this decision, then have it done in your own home, holding the dog in your arms and comforting it, so that its last memory is of your voice and your love. However painful it may be for you, you must not allow your dog to be dragged away to die in a strange place and without the company of those it has known and loved all its life.

We hope that for a long time before the end, your dog will enjoy a comfortable old age. Care in old age is really a matter of commonsense. The dog's bed needs to be a little warmer and softer than was required when it was a hardy youngster, and it needs a sensible diet that is easily digested and not too high in protein. While you should not allow your elderly Rott to become too fat, there is no reason why you should not allow the dog to enjoy its food and indulge in those little extra treats that it loves. As in humans, a little extra weight in old age is to be both expected and accepted.

Exercise of the older dog needs some thought. If you have an adequate exercising area, the dog will decide for itself when it feels like trotting around, and when it feels like a rest. If you do not have this facility, then you will have to take the dog for a walk as a part of its daily routine. However, it is important to remember that an easy journey for a young, fit dog may be a major effort for one that is feeling its age. Far too often, you see a fit man striding out on his evening constitutional, with an elderly dog plodding wearily behind. Remember, the dog is growing old more rapidly than you. You may argue that the dog expects and enjoys its walk – it may even fetch its lead as a reminder that it is time for 'walkies'. But dogs are creatures of habit, and you have ingrained this habit in the dog for the whole of its life. The dog should still have its walk, but make it a shorter one. If 'taking the dog for a walk' has become an excuse for a trip to the pub, then either find a closer pub, or a different excuse.

ENTROPION

This is a condition where the eyelids turn inwards causing the eyelashes to rub on the cornea, and this eventually causes ulcers. It is extremely painful for the dog, and there is no excuse for allowing your dog to suffer, as the corrective operation is simple and almost always successful. Mild entropion, although obvious to the knowledgeable, is often not diagnosed by the owner. Judges lose count of the number of times they are presented in the show ring with a dog with running, swollen eyes and the excuse that the dog had its head out of the car window during the trip to the show. Because the operation is simple and virtually undetectable, far too many breeders have perpetuated the condition by concealing that their stock has had surgery, and then continuing to breed from it. There is no excuse for this. We found that selective breeding can virtually eliminate entropion within very few generations.

SKIN TROUBLES

It is generally accepted that Rottweilers have thick skins, in both the figurative and literal senses. In spite of this they are extremely sensitive to insect bites and other skin irritations. A single flea-bite on a Rottweiler will cause the dog to nibble and scratch at the spot, and in a short time you will have a patch of wet eczema. Lack of attention will result in the rapid spread of the condition over a large area. This will become covered in pus, and the hair will eventually fall out. The first indication is usually a small patch of wet hair. Examine this, and you will find the first signs of eczema, often accompanied by signs of flea infestation. Obviously fleas are undesirable, but it is almost impossible to prevent your dog picking up the odd one. Clean bedding and regular use of an insect powder will help to reduce the problem.

However, there will almost certainly be a time when your Rott has eczema as we have described. We have found that vets tend to over-react to this problem. We frequently receive calls from owners complaining that their Rott has this condition and that the veterinary treatment is failing to cure it. The treatment given is usually in the form of an injection. We always give the same advice: first clean the area thoroughly with a diluted solution of antiseptic such as Dettol or Savlon, making sure that you remove all pus; then dry the area gently, and apply an ointment such as Germolene, which is both antiseptic and a local anaesthetic. The local anaesthetic helps to stop the dog aggravating the condition by further nibbling and scratching. In most cases this will quickly control the condition. The area will dry up, and you then have to be patient while the hair grows again. If your vet is sarcastic about this treatment, then we hope that you will be able to prove to him that it works – and in any case you can blame it on us!

RUPTURED CRUCIATE LIGAMENT

This is the rupture of the ligament which holds the stifle or knee joint together. It is often thought that this rupture can only occur by rapid movement, accompanied by the dog suddenly twisting or slipping. However, it is not unusual for it to occur when the dog is moving at a slow trot over a level surface, and this is almost certainly the result of a gradual stretching of the ligament over a period of time and eventually failing altogether. While rest and controlled exercise may cure the condition if the ligament is only strained, a complete rupture can only be cured by an operation to replace the ligament. The surgery is almost always successful, especially if it is done by a veterinary surgeon who has specialised in the problem. At present, there are varying opinions as to whether this condition, and the condition known as OCD (see next section), are hereditary. We are of the opinion that some bloodlines are more likely to suffer from one or both of these conditions than others, and for this reason we have never bred from stock that has suffered from either. It is also true to say that the Rottweiler's physical combination of agility, enthusiasm and weight means that it puts considerable strains and stresses on its body, and some of its orthopaedic problems can be attributed to this.

OSTEOCHONDRITIS DISSECANS (OCD)

This condition, usually abbreviated to OCD, comes about by the faulty development of bone and cartilage resulting in fragments dropping into the joint. The term is often used to cover a wide range of lameness in the shoulder, elbow, stifle and hock. It normally occurs in young dogs up to the age of about eighteen months. While vets are able to operate to cure the condition, the operation is not always successful, and while you should treat such lameness under veterinary supervision, it is probable that the condition will cure itself, given rest and patience. This condition may be hereditary, but there is also the possibility that it is caused by a diet deficiency, the excessive use of supplements such as vitamins or calcium, or a failure to absorb and convert food properly. Much more work needs to be done to establish whether modern diets or other living conditions are responsible for conditions such as this.

HIP DYSPLASIA (HD)

Much has been said and written on this subject during recent years. The fact that a number of very able people in various parts of the world have done a considerable amount of research on the subject and have evolved schemes for the control of HD has increased the prominence given to the problem. It must also be said that some of those who have done immensely valuable work in this field have allowed their determination to solve the problem to override other considerations, thus inflating the importance of the condition. At least one excellent bitch in Europe was not bred from for a number of years because of the difficulty of finding a suitable sire with good hips. The problem was not helped in Britain because the original HD scheme was a pass or fail scheme, which gave no indication to breeders whether a dog that had failed had only just missed a pass or whether it was hopelessly dysplastic. Neither did it take into account the possibility that hips that could be considered acceptable in one breed may be quite unacceptable in another. The current British BVA/KC scheme solves these problems. It produces a total score for each dog, enabling comparisons to be made between individual animals, and it also enables you to compare an individual score with the average score for the breed. At the time of writing the average score for Rottweilers is about 14. The best possible score is 0.0, with the worst possible being 106, or 53 for each hip.

While we agree that everything possible should be done to reduce and, if possible, eliminate HD, we consider that it should be assessed alongside the many factors to be taken into account when making decisions about breeding stock. It should not be allowed to take undue precedence over other factors. In our experience, HD is not a major problem in Rottweilers, provided that you are careful not to breed from stock that carries a high degree of HD in the bloodlines of both the sire and the dam. These are precautions that you should take with regard to any condition when making decisions about breeding. Many Rottweilers with quite high hip scores lead perfectly normal lives with no apparent disadvantages, and it is a matter for regret that many pet owners are caused unnecessary distress when they learn that their dog has HD, if it is not explained that their dog will probably not suffer in any way, and that it will lead a perfectly normal and full life.

The degree of HD that a dog may have is governed by both inheritance and environment. Most experts are of the opinion that the two elements affect the final condition in roughly equal parts. The statement that approximately 50 per cent of HD results from environmental factors does not eliminate the hereditary factor, or vice versa. The puppy will still inherit HD from its parents. It does, however, mean that the final severity of HD in the adult animal may be related to things which happen to it after it is born. No one has yet established precisely what environmental factors can affect the degree of HD, but it is assumed to include such things as injury at birth, slippery floors during rearing, weight, and diet.

Breeders cannot ignore HD: we need to be aware of it, and equally, to understand that it can be controlled and reduced by selective breeding. Breeders need to be honest both with themselves, and with those who buy their puppies and use their stud dogs. If you X-ray your breeding stock, and do not attempt to conceal stock that may have an unacceptably high score, then HD can become merely another breeding factor to be taken into account. As with entropion, the principal obstacle to solving the problem is that unscrupulous breeders are not willing to admit that there is a problem with their stock. The time has come for legislation to be agreed between the Kennel Club and the veterinary profession, making it compulsory for any vet, who either treats or diagnoses a hereditary condition, to report his findings to the parent body. These reports should be made available to the Kennel Club, and the findings should be published.

CANINE PARVOVIRUS (CPV)

Most of us who had been in dogs a long time had never heard of CPV before the early eighties. We knew all about distemper and hardpad, and thanks to the work of the drug companies, we felt that these killers of the past were no longer a problem. All you had to do was to make sure that your dogs had the routine inoculations. Death from distemper, once so common, just did not happen. We probably all became rather complacent. CPV, as far as is known, did not exist before 1977 and yet by the early eighties the whole of the dog world was in the grip of a major epidemic, with the loss of many dogs and puppies. The initial reaction of the drug companies was to adapt their existing vaccines, developed for cats, and to tell everyone that everything was under control. As far as most breeds were concerned, they were probably right. However, Rottweilers and also Dobermanns were in trouble. Dogs of these breeds who had the full course of inoculations were still going down with CPV, and frequently dying of it. Many breeders claimed that their dogs came home from the vet's surgery and became ill with parvo a few days later.

While this may have been coincidence, breeders rapidly became convinced that the Rottweiler was more vulnerable to CPV than other breeds. For some time this claim was disputed by both vets and the drug industry. It was even suggested that many of the owners of Rottweilers were temperamentally inclined to make a fuss, thus exaggerating the problem. The idea that one or more breeds should be more vulnerable than others was dismissed as rubbish. Gradually it began to be realised that the 'gut' reaction of Rottweiler breeders could have a basis in fact. Research on these lines began in Britain and was developed in the U.S.A. and elsewhere. The major work was reported in the U.S.A. by Lawrence T. Glickman and others in September 1985, using data from the Veterinary Hospital of the University of Pennsylvania and from the nationwide Veterinary Medical Data Program. Without going into all the technical explanations, this study clearly established that Rottweilers and also Dobermanns had significantly increased risks of canine parvovirus enteritis, and that there exist real differences in breed susceptibility to CPV. The paper made the point that the Rottweiler was one of the breeds that was used to develop the Dobermann, and claimed that both breeds have a high prevalence of von Willebrand's disease, the most common bleeding disorder in human beings and animals. In all our years of breeding dogs, we have never been aware of this prevalence, and in fact, we have never heard of a case in Rottweilers.

Once it was accepted that there was a very real problem as far as the Rottweiler and CPV was concerned, we began to make progress. In the U.K. the breakthrough came from a company called Intervet that not only developed a vaccine for use against CPV, but also carried out the bulk of their tests on Rottweilers. This product, under the name of Nobi-vac Parvo C, quickly showed that it was effective in protecting Rottweilers against CPV. One of the problems in vaccinating against CPV was the existence of the natural antibodies acquired by the puppy from its mother. The measurement of immunity is known as the titre level. As a rough guide, the puppy starts life with a titre level which is half that of its mother, and this decreases at the rate of half every ten days. The effect of the natural antibodies is to reject or neutralize the injected vaccine. You therefore have the risk of a dangerous gap in immunity between the loss of the natural antibodies and the immunity given by the injection. Nobi-vac C solved this problem by apparently overriding the natural antibodies, even when the injection was given as early as six weeks of age. At the same time we started to blood-test puppies at about nine to ten weeks of age to establish their titre level. To make absolutely sure, a second vaccination is now given at about twelve weeks, followed by a further blood test. Provided that a satisfactory titre level is then obtained, you should be reasonably certain that your Rottweiler is safe against CPV, and you only need to maintain this immunity by an annual booster. You may find, as we have, that the occasional dog refuses to develop an adequate titre level, usually considered to be about 500 to 1000. While this may be worrying, we have found that such animals seem to have an adequate immunity, even though, in theory, they are vulnerable.

In the past, we have always insisted that vaccination of our stock against CPV should be separate from vaccination against distemper, hardpad, leptospirosis and hepatitis. We felt that the 'cocktail' vaccination could have the effect of inhibiting the action of the vaccination against CPV. After all, parvo was the big problem, and we did not wish to do any thing which could affect our efforts at protection. Those who have done most of the research on this matter assure us that this is incorrect. They are confident that the combined vaccines are effective, and that the protection against CPV is not diminished in any way. It also has the advantage that, if used at six weeks, the puppy is protected against these other diseases from this age.

One final point on CPV. The use of Nobi-vac and the routines given above were successful in stopping the ravages of CPV during the latter half of the eighties. Recently there have been a number of reports that dogs, who have had the full routine of inoculations, have still contracted CPV and in some cases have died as a result. This raises the question as to whether the virus has mutated in some way or has become resistant to the present vaccines. Again, the experts tell us that this is not so. They also point out that there are other forms of gastric illness, and it is possible that these can be responsible for new cases, especially now that it has been established that Rottweilers may be more prone towards developing enteritis than other breeds. Certainly, the spectre of another killer similar to CPV is a worrying one for the breed. We can only hope that the scientists are looking at this, and if it does occur, they will be ahead of the game next time.